L.I.G.H.T.

(LIVING IN GOD'S HOLY TRUTH)

Discovering Your Identity through God's Preparation

L.I.G.H.T.

(LIVING IN GOD'S HOLY TRUTH)

NANCY FUJII

L.I.G.H.T. (Living in God's Holy Truth)
Copyright © 2020 by Nancy Fujii
All rights reserved.

Published in the United States of America by Credo House Publishers
a division of Credo Communications, LLC, Grand Rapids, Michigan
credohousepublishers.com

Unless otherwise indicated, Scripture quotations are from The Holy Bible,
English Standard Version, copyright © 2001 by Crossway Bibles,
a division of Good News Publishers. Used by permission. All rights reserved.

ISBN: 978-1-62586-183-2

Cover design by Jesus Cordero, Anointing Productions
Interior design and typesetting by Sharon VanLoozenoord
Editing by Elizabeth Banks and Christi McGuire

Printed in the United States of America

First edition

From mentor to loving memory,
this memoir is for you, Pearl.

AUTHOR'S NOTE

While this is a creative nonfiction work, all the events in this memoir are actual and not imaginary. I did not write to represent exact dialogue. Instead, I share memories that evoke an honest feeling and meaning of what I experienced. In all instances, the essence of my recollection is as accurate as possible, given my imperfect memory. The experiences I share in this book serve the story as it relates to my search for truth and love and how that led to discovering my identity and purpose. My goal is to share honest reflections with sensitivity not to condemn or criticize others involved in my experiences. For anonymity and privacy, sometimes, I do not mention proper names or gender.

CONTENTS

INTRODUCTION

If we only knew what we were made for.

Life offers two choices: Control or surrender. Do you strive for control and live for yourself, or do you surrender your life and live for God?

Few things awaken a soul more than a wayward life. On my quest for peace, I encountered a man who invited me to travel to an enchanted prison called heartland battleground, where he promised I would discover truth and freedom.

"What are you seeking?" he asked.

"I don't know," I told him.

"Come," he said, "if you follow me, you will see."

He was a peculiar sort, and I was skeptical, but my insatiable hunger to find truth and meaning amidst my midlife meandering provided an urgency to journey with this stranger. So, in every way that surrenders, I followed.

I quickly became accustomed to his "other way around" expressions. Down was up, last was first, dark was light, weak was strong, defeat was victory, and less was more.

His perceptions of the world were as captivating as they were confusing. But his language was not his only peculiarity. He lived unlike any other I had ever observed. His insights were more profound, and he had more joy than anyone I knew.

Everything I regarded as beautiful or valuable, he unraveled, only to create something infinitely more stunning and meaningful. He overcame conflict with peace, hatred with love, and lack with gratitude, teaching that one should never neglect children at their feet.

No one ever explained the matters of my heart to me the way this man did. His refreshing honesty pierced my soul. So much about my relationship with this man was indefinable. Nor could I describe what he had that I wanted. All I knew was I wanted all of it.

Had I finally met "the one" who could satisfy my lifelong, all-consuming discontent? I wanted to be patient. I didn't want to be wrong about this man as I was with others before him. And yet I knew there was something so uniquely extraordinary about him he was nothing like the others.

Our moments together turned into days, then weeks, then multiplied into years. So much time has passed since we met that I can't (or don't want to) remember much about my life before I knew him. What I know is that he fulfilled his promise. In my journey to the enchanted prison, I unearthed truth and freedom within my heartland battleground.

I want you to know the truth and experience freedom too. I hope you find it here, in this book, as you meet the same man I met so many years ago—the one I still love with all my heart and unequaled affection and, above all else, the one who won my heart.

His name is Jesus, and he wants to journey with you through your enemy-occupied enchanted prison, where you will encounter your soul and discover freedom within your heartland battleground.

You might think, "Oh, no! Not another fairy tale, feel-good book about faith and how knowing Jesus will change my life." To which I would say yes and no. Yes, this is a book about faith and Jesus. No, this book is not a fairy tale.

Jesus is a historical figure; he is not a myth. However, the aim of this book is not to provide evidence to convert atheists to Christianity. Countless historians and scholars have documented overwhelming proof for the historical Jesus.

In all fairness, I understand how easy it might be to think of Jesus as a fictional character in our culture today. Many people live as curated avatars on social media platforms, disguising their identity inside an imaginary person they want to look like and wish they were. But God is not like that. We do not make God up, and I will stake my life on that.

There is only one God, and Jesus Christ is uniquely his only son. God makes us in his image, and we root our identity in him. My unshakable faith in Jesus comes from the truth of the Bible. My confidence in the truth of the Bible and my undeniable proof that Jesus is real stands on how he changed my life. The story of Jesus, the Son of God, proves authentic and is life-giving. I don't need scientific proof.

Knowledge is a beautiful thing, but so is humility. God doesn't owe me an explanation for anything. If he doesn't reveal something to me, that's okay. God discerns what I need to know and what I don't. I trust he is wiser. Because of my love for Jesus, and how he transformed my life, I continue on this journey, one that I hope you will venture on.

This man, Jesus, spoke to me like no other. He described my heart more accurately than anyone who ever tried to teach me who I was, or how to live, or why my life mattered. He confronted and answered my most profound questions about loss, forgiveness, and trust while teaching me how to heal past wounds.

I spent time with Jesus and read his book, the Bible, to listen and learn about him. And just as I would have done with any other person who tried to win my trust, I had to decide. Would I trust and accept him as authentic or walk away from him believing he wasn't real?

I read the entire Bible and contemplated this man—the God-man Jesus Christ—and I cannot turn away from him. The eyewitness accounts of Jesus from Matthew, Mark, Luke, John, Paul, and Peter are in agreement and coherent. Furthermore, Jesus's early followers chose execution rather than recant that Jesus rose from the dead. Jesus's followers didn't make a silly mistake. Jesus really died on the cross, and Jesus's grave really was empty on the third day after his death. But more than all of this, my heart told me Jesus was real.

Jesus knows me far better and is much wiser than my biological parents—the people who raised me hypocritically to their lives. And Jesus knows me more intimately and is much more knowledgeable than my family-by-marriage, who believe that avoiding shame proves the best way to live. And it is Jesus who knows me far better and is so much more sensible than what any positive psychology or acceptance and coping therapy may offer.

Morally confused and living in a state of perpetual want and need for more, my heart ached for beauty and value. To quench this irresistible yearning, I listened to people who were chock-full of unsolicited advice for how I should live my life, and when their suggestions didn't work, I tried self-will.

I roamed west to east and back again, traveled cross-country, and climbed each cascading disappointment until I could no longer endure. Only when I searched my soul and reached for something bigger and wiser than myself—God—did my inexhaustible search end. Confronted with a choice, I chose Jesus.

We weave God into every part of our lives and the created order of our world, including man, nature, and creatures. God speaks to us through his creations. How can I not believe in God while driving through breathtaking icicle-frosted waterfalls on a narrow winding road leading to a majestic snow-covered mountain? And how can I not believe in God beholding the vast Pacific Ocean with crashing waves on a boardwalk beach surrounding quaint seaside villages?

How can I not believe in God gazing at an expansive sky surrounding a glowing moon and bright stars, squinting at radiant sunbeams, or sitting awestruck from my porch swing pondering the beauty of the red maple tree blooming in my yard? And what should I think as I watch my labradoodle puppy retrieve and devour prey, not by command but by instinct?

If you have given birth or seen a child's birth, how can you not believe in God? How can I not believe in God when I see his majestic beauty and divine creativity? His infinitely glorious goodness is everywhere I turn.

But he doesn't stop at creating. He makes all things work together for good. He is the master sculptor carving the puzzle pieces in our lives. Through our pain and pleasures and our strengths and weaknesses, God is forming our life stories. But our stories are, in reality, all his story. It's HIStory in the making.

May God's will be done, not my will be done. I can now reflect on events that happened years ago and understand why it happened the way it did. The beauty of our lives is that God is designing and directing our stories.

Knowing God through a personal relationship with him proved different from the religion of my childhood. The blind eyes of my heart were open to a light that brought me freedom. Only God can open the eyes of our hearts and bring light to the darkness. And all at once, the invisible becomes visible, the secret known. God reveals the hidden, and the shadows turn to light. As Jesus stood before me, it was as if he had always been there.

How can blind people know Jesus? The apostle Paul's eyes were blind on the road to Damascus. His conversion came through the eyes of his heart. I, too, saw (and still see) Jesus this way. And, like Paul, I always want to be with Jesus. We need the eyes of our hearts open to see God.

Eyes see facts, not truth. Doubting Thomas, the apostle, refused to believe that the resurrected Jesus appeared to the other apostles until he could touch and see the wounds received by Jesus on the cross.

> Then he [Jesus] said to Thomas, "Put your finger here, and see my hands; and put out your hand, and place it in my side. Do not disbelieve, but believe." Thomas answered him, "My Lord and my God!" Jesus said to him, "Have you believed because you have seen me? Blessed are those who have not seen and yet have believed." (John 20:27–29)

Before the light of Jesus came into my heart, I had an extreme anti-God state of mind. My spirit was rebellious. Rigid religious rituals and beliefs did not ring true through my experiences. I was skeptical of anything science could not verify. I didn't want to trust or accept something I didn't understand. Hung up on facts, I was missing the significance.

I met Jesus in 2011. I could not describe what happened to me when I met him, but today I can. Now my only burden, and the goal of this book, is to share his truth with you.

How do I know God and the Bible are true? God designs our hearts to connect with him and others through his truth and love. One way he speaks to us is in our experiences with him and through our experiences with others. Everything about our lives weaves into God's story. He is the way, the truth, and the life (John 14:6).

People either live in the light, or they live in darkness. The most important question of our lives is: Do I live for God, or do I live for myself? The Bible teaches us to take up our cross and follow Jesus: "Then Jesus told his disciples, "If anyone would come after me, let him deny himself and take up his cross and follow me" (Matthew 16:24).

How do we do that? We love God, we love others, and we deny ourselves. But why would we do that? Because God promises that we will find greater joy in him than in the things we deny.

I wrote this book in three parts: My Story, God's Story, and Our Story. In "My Story" I share pieces of my past to help understand God's story through mine. "God's Story" shows how our identity in Christ leads to purpose and helps us understand relationships and forgiveness, culminating in living a lasting legacy. "Our Story" shows how Jesus is part of our collective story and that the meaning of our lives is to connect to God and reflect him to others.

I long to share God's truth with you. My prayer is that God opens your heart's eyes to consider these insights so you can experience the same freedom I did when L.I.G.H.T. (Living in God's Holy Truth) led me to discover my identity through God's preparation.

Living in God's holy truth set me free from self-destruction, guilt, shame, fear, isolation, people-pleasing traps, and trivial life pursuits. Knowing Jesus frees me from pride and an unforgiving heart. I cannot imagine anyone who does not want that kind of freedom.

I close where I began asking if you surrender your life and live for God, or do you seek to control your life and live for yourself? Free will lets me decide which one I choose and allows you to decide for yourself.

By God's grace, your freedom awaits.

PART ONE

MY STORY

CHAPTER ONE

MY STORY

Abuse and fear plagued my childhood. My past life was fraught with danger. I saw and experienced things growing up that I've tried hard to forget.

Decades of distance from my former life brings me clarity that I could not have had when these events occurred. I now have words to describe what I can only imagine my immature mind must have thought and how I felt.

Grappling with hard-to-love parents, unending disappointments, and deep shame and guilt, life was confusing and unstable for my young self. Obscured by scandal inside my less than ideal background, I spent most of my childhood nursing insecurities and fighting battles that I didn't know how to win.

A childhood infected with abuse hindered my ability to discern the truth. I looked for love, but none came. Scared and alone, I trusted no one. My only option was survival. Survival through physical and psychological trauma defined me in unimaginable ways with damaging effects.

Family had always been my highest value. My childhood dream was to marry a wonderful man, a farmer actually, and have a loving family with lots of kids. So what do you do when your family shatters your dream and exploits your innocence?

I'm guessing that we all have people in our lives we like enough to want to extend love and kindness to them. The people you want to be most loving toward would likely be people you grew up with and feel closest to—your family. I don't think many would argue that desirable family characteristics are honest, nurturing, healthy, and safe—this is the family I wanted. But I didn't grow up in this family. And I didn't like many people that were part of my family.

Past suffering led me to search for truth and someone to love. Questions like, "What's the purpose of my life? Why is there suffering? Why am I here?" left me hopelessly wandering through a painful life of perpetual inconsequence. A spiritual journey to find my identity and reason to live turned what I knew about God upside down.

I broke loose from the shackles of selfish pride and control to discover my identity and meaning of life. I learned what it means to be human. To live well and suffer well. I learned what it means to have joy in sorrow and taste and feel life in the fullest sense, to be free.

God is preparing me in this life for the next. Before professing my faith, I will share parts of my past to help you understand God's story through mine. I pray that God's grace stirs your soul as you read how these parallel dimensions of my life diverged and then converged to bring truth and love that helped me discover my true identity at long last. To this beginning, I now turn.

CHAPTER TWO

FORMATIVE YEARS

Born in 1959 and raised in Illinois, I grew up with three brothers. We lived near the West Side in Chicago, one of the most dangerous parts of the city where crime, violence, drugs, and alcohol ravaged neighborhoods with aftershock effects.

My parents sent my siblings and me to Catholic Catechism classes at a young age to learn about God, which confused me because my parents did not practice the Catholic teachings. The moral landscape was vacant in our home.

I remember my formative years in ways I don't want to. Specific memories come with a price. One way to reflect on these memories is to blame my parents and the Catholic Church for past wounds and disappointments. But why would I do that?

I don't want to vilify my parents for the way I turned out, nor do I want to desecrate the Catholic Church because I lacked one thing or another that may have been more helpful to lead me on a path of least resistance. The memories I share now serve as a reference point in my search for truth and love.

My parents married young and wasted no time having children. My mom had an older brother and sister. My maternal grandparents were alive throughout my childhood. My mom was the quintessential "Daddy's Little Girl." She married my dad when she was eighteen years old and had four children by age twenty-three.

When I reached the age of reasoning, I realized my mom and I valued life differently. So much of her behavior was distasteful and disturbing to me. She was a delusional and self-absorbed woman starved for attention who lived vicariously through me, her only daughter.

Everything my mom did, she did for attention. She never entered or left a room unnoticed. I remember my mom openly flirting with men, speaking in sexual innuendos, and grabbing their private parts. In restaurants, she often leaned over another person's plate of food and, without permission, jabbed her fork in part of their meal and ate it, letting them know how wonderful it was to taste what they were eating.

Whenever she ordered iced tea, she made it a point to request "extra, extra, extra," lemon. Did she not know the meaning of the word extra, or was she trying to ensure her order came back correct because the server might have been hearing impaired? I think it was merely a pathetic need for attention. Whatever the reasons, her brazen attitude and unsophisticated behaviors were embarrassing.

My mom was also a hypochondriac. She rarely drank alcohol, but at one point, a doctor prescribed Valium (considered "Mother's Little Helper" in those days) for one of her ailments. I'm guessing she enjoyed how it made her feel because she often took the pills. I could never experience a genuine connection or a meaningful relationship with my mom, either in my younger years or my adult life.

My dad had three siblings. His dad died before I was born, but I knew his mom in my early childhood. Dad was the only person in his immediate family to graduate from college, becoming a successful business owner.

Like his dad, my dad was, though he would never admit it, an alcoholic. My dad did two things exceptionally well: work and rage. He never addressed me in a quiet voice when he had something to say that was wrong, either about me or his life. I knew his anger and authority well.

His temper seemed fueled by an intense desire for vengeance and punishment, always looking for a fight, wanting to hurt someone without thinking or caring about the consequences. He seemed to have an emotional need to dominate and control others, which he did with biting criticism, belittlement, and sarcasm. Growing up, I remember him as an alcoholic tyrant with explosive rage.

When I was around seven years old, my mom told me my dad was going away on vacation with my grandfather. I would later learn their vacation spot was a prison. My grandfather and dad became entangled in a crime my uncle masterminded. Somehow my uncle evaded a prison sentence.

I remember visiting my uncle's house almost every Sunday with my family. My uncle liked to hold court, occupying his throne at a long stately table surrounded by his minions—criminals, prostitutes, alcoholics, and drug addicts. The room had the stench of alcohol, and the air was thick with cigarette smoke and vulgar language. Occasionally I would wander away from his stage for a little fresh air.

My uncle had multiple sclerosis and couldn't drive, so he bought a limousine and hired someone to chauffeur him. My uncle invited his limo driver, allegedly a convicted pedophile, to live in his basement. He shared the basement with my teenage cousin, who had not been sober in years.

My uncle's ex-wife occupied the third floor of his house. Once I visited her upstairs, I saw her tie a strap-like item (it looked like a small rubber belt) to her arm and watched her shoot a needle into her swelled veins. I later learned this was to feed her amphetamine addiction. Another cousin who shared the apartment upstairs was a teenage single mom, impregnated by my uncle's best friend, who came to live in his home following his parole.

My uncle kept company with sketchy men who demoralized women with aggression and manipulation. I remember hearing on television news that police discovered a man, whom my uncle frequently associated with, stabbed and strangled, lying dead in a car's trunk.

My uncle was my sexual abuser. My dad and my uncle terrified me, for different reasons, but as a child, I had no defense and nowhere to run. Almost every male figure in my life represented wrath, neglect, and danger, including my brothers who, for reasons unclear to me, would strip my dolls naked, tie them to basement posts, and beat them with a belt buckle. My mom and aunt were the only prominent women in my life, and neither of them were exactly role-model material.

My mom found a part-time receptionist job while my dad was away. She spent mornings working and afternoons prancing around town with her friends. After my dad returned from his vacation, he started a new business where he spent long hours in the office and less time at home.

When my parents had time off from work, they globe-trotted on cruises and safaris, leaving their child-rearing responsibilities to an older woman they met through the church who provided live-in childcare for a nominal fee. This woman cooked, and cleaned, and sewed, and was more present in my life than my parents. She made hamburgers with oatmeal and planted used tea bags in the dirt surrounding our backyard.

One day I wanted to help her with household chores, so I offered to do laundry. She followed me to the basement and saw me unfold and climb a ladder resting against a wall next to the washer. I needed the ladder to reach the metal pull chain attached to the lightbulb hanging from the ceiling.

The next time I went to do laundry, the pull chain had a long, thin string tied to the chain cord with a button at the end. The line reached me at eye level, so yanking the button at the end of the string was all I had to do to see the room light up. No ladder required.

This woman was a gem. I loved her deeply. She favored my younger brother over my two older brothers and me, but I didn't mind. My younger brother had a rare childhood condition that affected his hip. He was in a wheelchair most of his childhood until he advanced to crutches.

I think she was so fond of him because she was a woman well acquainted with suffering. Our parents told us she lived with her brother, who beat her. I got the impression it was on a fairly regular basis.

Unfortunately, this precious soul was old and ill, and her influence in my life was brief. The last time I saw her, she was lying in a bed dying in a nursing home. I wondered how many people visited her in her last days and if anyone cared about her. I did.

As I write this, I realize how my affections for this dear woman have escaped me all these years, and now, inside this intimate wandering, I'm struck with a troubling sense of loss. She was a caring and loving woman with a humility that attracted me. She could very well have been the first person I ever loved. This memory echoes of a broken heart never healed.

Attending church only on Christmas and Easter, the religious classes I attended with my brothers prepared me to receive the Catholic sacraments of Penance, Holy Communion, and Confirmation. Somewhere in my adolescence, a day came when (with head bowed, eyes closed, and hands folded) I kneeled for the last time in a dark confessional booth and remorsefully whispered those frightful words, "Bless me, Father, for I have sinned." And that was the end of that. I became an ex-Catholic.

I vowed from that day forward that I would no longer struggle to please God or be hostage to my intense guilt because I could never merit his favor. It seemed a simple way to end my guilt. But things didn't work out as I planned.

CHAPTER THREE

FAMILY IDENTITY

Though understanding my feelings and motives at this young age with perfect memory is impossible, I imagine the abruptness of losing my childhood innocence left me fearful and angry. Trying to make sense of my troubled family, I no longer had a home; I had a battleground. I unwillingly became an intense kid, a tiny warrior dedicated to exposing the truth behind the lies by reading expressions and body language. I imagine I thought this hypervigilant detection of manipulation would protect me.

In reflection, I can see how honing these skills could make it easier for me to deceive others because survival often meant posing and suppressing my genuine feelings to avoid another person's wrath. Learning to manipulate others was an unintended consequence of my resilience.

By my teenage years, I was associating my identity with my family's values and behaviors, and my hometown Chicago's reputation. I lived the life my family modeled. I became one of many who lived through—and ultimately contributed to—the abuse cycle within my family.

After attending my first year of high school in my hometown, my family moved from the West Side of Chicago, to a more prominent suburb northwest of the city where I began my second year of high school. My father's absence from home was more noticeable during my teenage years.

My mom, no longer working, joined social clubs in our new town, where the women met for lunch and played card games at each other's houses. My parents often hosted parties inviting family and friends with alcohol and marijuana in abundant supply. I began smoking pot, drinking, and trying my mom's Valium pills. I did not ask to be born into this family, but I was, I suppose, doing my best to adapt to it.

My mom had an affair during my high school years. She and I moved out of our house to live with my uncle for a brief period. I vaguely remember conversations about divorce, but ultimately my parents reconciled, and my mom and I moved back home. During the temporary separation, my mom went on a shopping spree, buying clothes and a car, and I'm not sure what else, charging every credit card she could find in my dad's name to the limit.

As a child, I feared my dad. As an adult, I felt a peculiar aggravation toward him. It was disturbing and uncomfortable to be around my dad. He rarely shared his heart with anyone, but he did with me, mainly when he drank, which made me feel like the object of his need for intimacy unattainable from anyone else. I felt deeply connected to my dad because he shared so much about himself with me, but I also felt profoundly misunderstood and violated.

My association with my uncle continued for years beyond my youth through adulthood. I remember being fond of my uncle growing up, perhaps because my dad idolized him, but now the word that always comes to mind when I think of my uncle is sinister. Time and maturity show me now how distorted and perverse my affections for him were. I didn't, however, know then what I know now.

It was around this time I remember learning that my youngest brother had Schizophrenia. My brother had unusual behavior, which was hard to detect in my family, that manifested over time to this diagnosis. My parents thought his childhood hip disease contributed to his strange behavior, so they ignored it for a long time.

Chaos and instability filled my adolescent and teenage years until the day I ran away from home. I spent a few harrowing nights on my own before returning home to finish high school. A strong neediness (for what I didn't understand) persisted that, try as I might, I couldn't ignore. Filled with an indiscernible longing and constant fear of danger made my quest for truth and love more urgent.

My school grades deteriorated, and I lost interest in all subjects. I was a horrible student. Adding to my low self-esteem was my disappointment that I was part of an incredibly messed up family. Kids began bullying me at school because I was different. The fighter in me was morphing to bolder and more obnoxious and provocative behaviors, just like my mom. I was spinning out of control, but I didn't know how to stop it.

Not feeling academically gifted in the traditional sense, I relied on my instincts and ability to adapt and learn quickly. It wasn't long before I realized education beyond high school was not an option for me. Life, it appeared, would be my classroom.

A younger sister of a classmate and I forged a friendship, becoming inseparable in the year following my high school graduation. On the outside, my friend's family appeared intact. In reality, her family life was a mess—drinking, drugs, mental illness, deceit, divorce. All of it affected her. I felt a kindred connection to her.

Desperate to be free of our family troubles, we boarded a plane to California. When we got there, we rented a clean room at the YMCA, and I quickly found a waitress job to take care of our living expenses.

Without a car, my girlfriend and I hitchhiked to get around. We met a Native American Indian on one of our hitchhiking excursions. He worked as a meat cutter for a local grocery store. He had an eagle tattooed on his chest and drank canned screwdriver cocktails. Like my father, he did two things well—work and rage. Also, like my father, he drank . . . a lot.

My girlfriend and I enjoyed our free-spirited life until the day she experienced something like a nervous breakdown. I called her brother, who planned to pick up his sister and take her to a hospital for evaluation.

After my girlfriend left, I spent most of my free time after working my waitress job with my new California friend (the one we met hitchhiking). He, too, much like my girlfriend and I, harbored a rebellious free spirit.

One day, somewhat randomly, my friend and I ventured on a day trip to Tijuana, Mexico. I remember threading through the crowded streets where people bartered and sold goods. Mexican pinatas and native woven blankets hung over the storefront entrances. Inside the stores, sequin Mariachi sombreros, trinkets, silver jewelry, leather jackets, and velvet paintings of Jesus were for sale.

I recall going into one of these stores, where my friend suggested, out of the blue, we get married. I'm guessing I must have thought it was a good idea because that's what we did. Exactly why I might have thought it was a good idea eludes me, but I would soon learn it wasn't.

I remember my friend guiding me to a room inside the store and speaking Spanish to a man sitting behind a desk. After answering some questions, the man produced a marriage certificate requiring our signatures. We were not in an official civil or registry office, and I don't remember presenting anything to validate my identity. I don't recall taking the event too seriously because I was skeptical if it was legal.

It wasn't long before I became a victim of domestic violence. A broken home, abuse survivor, inevitable statistic? Perhaps, but I could not have had the maturity or wisdom to know that then. After the abuse, I would drink to anesthetize the horror.

To escape my home life, I enrolled in a local certification program to learn how to use a typewriter and to take shorthand. These skills provided me with more lucrative opportunities for employment and brought me a respite from home.

Months passed inside cycles of abuse and generous amounts of tequila. A day came when I got word from Chicago that my younger, Schizophrenic brother was on a plane to California to live with me. The memory of this time in my life is fuzzy. However, there is one day that seems less vague than others.

I remember I was driving, with my brother sitting next to me in the passenger seat, and I swerved to avoid something in the road. We spun out of control for several minutes before the car miraculously stopped on the freeway's shoulder—without a scratch. Perhaps I remember this because it was a wake-up call to my wild life.

My brother advanced from marijuana to shooting drugs. Another vague memory is the day my brother excused himself to leave the room and then I heard a thud against his door. Upon opening it, I found him convulsing on the floor, foaming at the mouth from an overdose. Encounters with my younger brother were always fearful and disturbing, which only added to my troubled and reckless life. Eventually, I called my family to let them know my brother needed to return home.

Some months later, I learned my oldest brother, who just graduated from college and was engaged, had been in a fatal car accident in Chicago. After graduation, he had begun working for my uncle. On the night he died, he was drinking with my uncle until the early morning and drove my uncle to his house after the partying ended. After dropping my uncle at his house, and while driving himself home on Lake Shore Drive, he fell asleep at the wheel, crossing the median where oncoming cars from the opposite direction piled up, hitting his car head on in a fatal collision.

Not having much of a relationship with my older brother growing up, we were not close. He was my dad's and grandparent's favorite— the "most likely to succeed," smart, handsome, and full of promise for a bright future.

I returned home for my brother's memorial. During my visit, I went to his apartment and discovered a shoebox of keepsakes in his closet. Rummaging through, I found a wedding card addressed to me. I don't remember the words, but I sensed the tender sentiment he wrote was obligatory. I pondered for the longest time why he never mailed it. Initially, I recall thinking he most likely didn't send it because his feelings were insincere.

Then another possibility occurred to me. I considered my brother could have been so troubled by my out-of-control lifestyle that he felt conflicted about how best to help his little sister. Maybe instead of mailing the card, he would fly to California and rescue me. The longer I thought about this, the more I convinced myself that I was only secretly hoping my brother could have been the one positive role model for me to remember from my family. Desperately wanting someone to save me, he could be the hero in my life that he was to so many others.

Even though I wasn't close to my brother, his death brought a profound sadness to my heart. I struggled with survivor guilt after his accident, wondering how such a well-liked and presumably good person could die so young when someone like me was more deserving of a premature death.

Shortly after we buried my brother, I returned to my life in California. It was only weeks later that I learned my mom was in a debilitating, near-fatal car accident, severely injured and disfigured. She was distraught over losing her son and tried to kill herself by driving her car into a tree. My dad asked if I would return home to nurse her back to health. I did.

I cared for my mom for several months in Chicago before returning to my California life. I think, but I don't know this for sure, I must have felt vulnerable around my family in Chicago when I was there, but returning to California could not have felt much different. I continued to look for significance in my work, which distracted me from the domestic violence in my home.

Not long after my mom's car accident, I learned she suffered a mild stroke. Expecting a quick and full recovery, my dad asked me to return home to care for my mom during her rehabilitation. Again, I boarded a plane back to Chicago, but this time, I did something different. Before returning to Chicago, I met with an attorney in California to end my marriage.

It was never clear to me then if marriage in Tijuana was legal in other countries. Still, I proceeded with a dissolution of my marriage. Whatever label I attach to the relationship is irrelevant now. It was a mess, and it ended.

In reflection, it's not that I didn't care because, despite my reckless abandon, I don't think I have ever been an insensitive person. Perhaps more accurately, underneath the false bravado and deep emotional wounds, there was a compassionate person.

I didn't know what to make of my life at this stage. Twenty-two years old and spinning out of control, I was just as confused, unstable, fearful, and angry as I was in my childhood. I thought about my girlfriend, who went to the hospital, and though I would see her periodically for several years, she never regained a healthy mental state.

It was around this time that my youngest brother went psychotic. I remember receiving the news that he was on and off medication and living in a treatment center in Chicago when he told a psychiatrist he wanted to kill my mother. After attacking and injuring a nurse where he was living, a court order sent him to a maximum-security mental health facility.

Armed with a resolve to find a better life, I left California and returned to Chicago. Convinced that nothing good could ever come from my family, I was determined to find a new identity. My plan was a simple one. After my mom's recovery, I would remove myself from any association with my family and reinvent a new identity—an improved version of me. I thought all I had to do was physically separate myself from my family, which didn't seem difficult given my fiercely independent nature.

Ignorant yet somehow aware, I was gradually beginning to realize I had an impossible problem—what was beneath my family's filth was me. Forced to admit the many ways I had become like my family, my plans to disassociate myself from them and reinvent a new identity came crashing down, and I had no choice but to run for shelter from the storm.

CHAPTER FOUR

WORK IDENTITY

From coast to coast, I poured myself into what would ultimately amount to a thirty-year career in the corporate world. With nothing more than a high school diploma, my career was a climb. Eventually, through hard work and career advancement, I progressed from entry-level to six-figure management positions.

Desperate for acceptance and praise, I became passionate about lifelong learning and continually strived for self-improvement. This passion, coupled with the birth of the Internet in 1983, provided me with vast opportunities to broaden my skills through technology and software certification training.

The accolades and awards I received at work gave me a new identity. Recognized as competent, responsible, and trustworthy, I finally felt seen and heard, having significance and appreciation from others. This tiny warrior was morphing into a ninja workhorse. A woman I worked for once told me I could slow down a bit. She said the goal was not to clear my inbox of newly added projects before I left every day. I remember thinking, how absurd!

While living independently of my parents, I worked as an executive assistant for a Fortune 500 company. I continued with job-related training in this firm, earning several promotions and landing an assignment to work overseas in Europe.

As the steps on the corporate ladder increased, so did the egos and corruption. Coworkers were competing, and executives were manipulating, each trying to gain an advantage over the next person. I found little ethical behavior or love in the cutthroat business world.

By now, I was a high-functioning alcoholic—organized, efficient, and accomplished on the outside, but chaotic and self-destructive underneath. As a polite, professional perfectionist, committed to continuous self-improvement that advanced my career, I could deny the many ways alcohol was destroying my life.

During after-work happy hours, many occasions hinted that my drinking was a problem, but I framed them as isolated incidents and did my best to hide my struggles and keep up my stellar work ethic. Living a double life, I concealed my nonwork persona from my professional one. Career advancement, let alone employment, were not attainable if my employers knew about my troubled life and family's social ills. I mean, how would that interview go?

Interviewer: "Tell me about yourself, your strengths, and your weaknesses."

Me: "Okay, well, my highest education is high school. I barely graduated because I was such a poor student. I'm a broken-home abuse survivor who drinks way more than I should to numb myself from the inescapable recurring nightmares I have of the enduring deviant and destructive behaviors I was exposed to and subsequently contributed to inside my family. In a nutshell, I'm a hot mess. My weaknesses are too many to mention in the time we have for this interview. My strengths are two: I'm a quick learner, self-taught at everything I know, and can clear an inbox faster than a hungry dog can lick his plate clean. So, when can I start?"

Of course, I couldn't share that, so instead, I persevered through hard work, telling them what they wanted to hear while covering the truth. The political correctness of the corporate culture troubled me. It reminded me of the delusion and deception prevalent in my past life, where values became situational to justify motives and rationalize behavior. I was miserable inside.

My only outlet to this masquerade party was my personal life, which was becoming increasingly difficult to manage and even harder not to recognize the similarity it bore to my professional life. I was drinking my way to denial well beyond reason.

My childhood and Catholic upbringing produced years of shameful memories and unhealthy religious guilt. I spent much of my early life hiding secrets. I kept my secrets from everyone, including myself, because secrets hurt and secrets haunt.

My past life taught me you are only as sick as your secrets. The more you hide, the sicker you become, and the only people who are impressed with posers are other posers. Confession was healing, and sharing my life helped me connect with others, but the people I confided in found running away more comfortable than listening to the truth about my background or caring about me.

I often felt judged when I shared my heart, so I only allowed a few people in those authentic places. Lacking trust isolated me from others, which prevented me from experiencing healthy relationships. The struggle for me was sharing my whole heart with people who didn't care about me or my welfare and getting nothing in return. My resolve to tuck away my heartache and press on would have been fine if I didn't have a conscience bent on telling the truth.

I longed for rules and structure and dreamed of a place where people respected, encouraged, accepted, and loved each other the way they were. But in this daunting pursuit, even after freeing myself from the toxic lifestyle associated with my family, I found myself in a cesspool of immorality and treachery within my work and friend circles.

After my position in Europe was over, I returned to Chicago and found another Fortune 500 job. I worked for several more years in Chicago, building my career identity while trying to reconcile the personal, messed-up me through alcohol and psychotherapy.

Drinking and counseling temporarily numbed me to the reality of my brokenness, but neither cured me. After every disappointment, I kept telling myself to hang on, saying I will, someday, find the truth and love. My dreams became my hope and reason for keeping on.

Growing up in fear taught me to fight. A racing heart, difficulty breathing, overwhelming fear—perceived danger typically triggers a fight-or-flight response. I fought to survive, in part, I think, because I had nowhere to go, feeling captive in a place I wanted to conquer.

Fearful of unwanted consequences, I internalized simmering anger and deep wounds throughout my childhood. Forced to live with people I didn't like, I was angry and distrusting. I thought parents were supposed to protect children from danger, not expose them to it. Neglected, rejected, and unprotected, I was hurt.

Though I don't recall having a precise moment when I hit bottom, realizing my work and family identities were inseparable motivated me to return to California. When the time came for me to spread my wings, I took flight—literally. Reducing my life to one suitcase, I boarded a plane back to California and left my life in Chicago behind. Farewell shattered dreams; hello picture-perfect loving family and new identity. Or so I thought.

CHAPTER FIVE

MARRIAGE IDENTITY

Early in life moral injuries formed my self-worth. Soaring forward with positive self-esteem meant restraining disturbing and painful childhood memories to avoid reliving the trauma. Underneath the externally confident, professional, and social persona lived the internal, authentically suppressed real me. And she was screaming, "Let me out!" These warring identities confused me. Struggling to find healthy boundaries between these two tensions, and surrounded by duplicity, I couldn't find a way out.

I wanted love, so I sought it. My lifestyle invited negative attention that left me contorting myself into a people-pleasing pretzel. I lacked discretion and discernment about what healthy relationships were. When my dependence shifted to independence, and I could run from harm, my response turned from fight to flight. I vowed never again to get close to anyone who could hurt me. Trust and tolerance were not in my economy. If someone hurt me, I cut them out of my life. Any sense of repeating traumatic experiences was a weight I could not carry.

Experience proved finding employment would not be difficult. As I began my job search, I strategized how to untangle the associations between my professional and personal life. Making progress meeting people who were an improvement over previous relationships, I found a position working for a corporate executive known for his integrity and loyalty to his employees and business relationships. Unlike so many former executives I worked for, he was humble, honest, and compassionate.

We worked together for a year before we began dating. When our relationship became personal, I left the company to work elsewhere. Within a few years, our careers moved both of us to the East Coast. While living and working in Manhattan, we became engaged.

After we were engaged, I met his family for the first time. It delighted me to meet his parents, siblings, extended family, and three daughters he had from a previous marriage. His daughters were twenty-five, twenty-three, and twenty-one years old when I met them.

It appeared I finally found truth and love. I met the man of my dreams and became part of a family I always wanted. My husband's family had a much different pedigree than mine—educated and non-abusive people with a moral compass. I was sure this family would bring me genuine love and a new identity, but I was wrong.

Willing but unprepared, I wholeheartedly gave my life to my fiancé (Mike) and his family. After we announced our engagement, his mom invited me to visit her in California. Planning to stay through the winter holidays, I arrived for my visit with one travel bag.

Two weeks after I arrived, Mike's mom suffered a mild stroke. Lying on a gurney in the hospital emergency room, she gripped our hands and pleaded with Mike and me not to leave her. So we didn't, and I never saw my Manhattan apartment again. Mike handled moving our personal effects coast-to-coast, and we bought a home where I lived with Mike and his mom. I quit working to become my soon-to-be mother-in-law's primary caregiver.

Initially, there was blended family harmony as Mike's daughters and other family members accepted me with warmth and kindness. And I recall great mutual joy over an intimate bond between Mike's mom and me when she became the beloved mother I longed for, and I became the adored daughter she never had.

Joyful times were short-lived, though, and soon my new family began expressing intense dislike for me. I remember some treating me with hostile silence while others aggressively maligned me. After our marriage, Mike and his mom were the only ones accepting me.

The love and affection I felt from Mike and his mom seemed genuine, but the swift and vicious rejection I experienced from the rest of Mike's family felt hateful and undeserved. The alienation was devastating. Seldom were my encounters with these family members happy. They evoke a somewhat different memory for me. There were too many possibilities to know why this happened, so Mike and I sought professional help to find answers.

Our therapist educated us on the myriad of negative consequences divorce has on children, pointing out children's overwhelming emotional needs, regardless of their age. These practical insights proved helpful to us. Our counselor suggested we engage other family members in our sessions, so we did. Our efforts to bring other family members into open and honest communication with the stepfamily issues we were all experiencing were unsuccessful in the long term, so instead, we invited others to share their concerns at home in periodic family meetings. Mike also met continually with his daughters separate from me, pleading with them to consider having a cordial relationship with me.

I continued with professional counseling individually with my therapist for several months. Though I was learning much about myself and the possible reasons for his family's behaviors toward me and my unhealthy responses to them, I couldn't fully understand or embrace change without others' honesty or accountability. Without a willingness to acknowledge and accept another person's feelings, peacemaking became impossible.

I tried hard to ignore the negative words and vulgar attitudes I continued to receive from Mike's family throughout my months in therapy. Still, my coping methods let me down, and I hit an emotional wall of self-defense. I recall feeling conflicted trying to handle these encounters as graciously as possible and feeling like I didn't want to live through another family heartbreak. It wasn't long before Mike would find me shrinking, trembling in a corner, hugging my knees and sobbing.

On one occasion, after a family member attacked me verbally, I fled. I was afraid to go back to our home because Mike was out of town, so I checked into a hotel. My mother-in-law was in the hospital again, so going home meant I would have been alone, and I feared this family member would come into my house and continue with the emotional abuse.

The screaming words from this family member's explosive rage reverberated through my soul. The ugly words hurled at me played in my head like a broken record, and the expressed anger that came with it terrified me. Not only were those harsh words torpedoing in my head, but I was reliving all the trauma from my dad's rage so many years before.

When my fight turned to flight, and I became independent of my parents, I realized that fighting was not the best way to respond to conflict, but running from it was no better. Conflict revealed my brokenness, so I avoided it by running to conceal it. Feeling hopeless, I wanted to bury my hurt and shame. I tried to deny and lie about what was wrong.

The dysfunctional chaos and infighting continued as relational divisions within my new family became broader and more profound. One day amidst all of this, I overhead Mike telling his mom something to the effect that I was different and would always be an outcast from their family.

Although I see things differently now, I could only see it then as an ultimate betrayal, and this dishonesty was more than I could handle. I imagine I froze, trying to process what was happening as I calculated plans for a quick escape. I must have gathered what I thought I would need to break free from this perceived evil person and his entire family. I ended up in my car, driving away from my home, to where I didn't know.

Beyond devastated, I felt so utterly hopeless that I wanted to end my life. Life shaped at the hands of abusers taught me to live by hope, and even in a sense, by faith. Though hope can live as a powerful force in my heart, it is also fragile and can crumble quickly. My longings and limitations emptied me. More than heartbroken, I was tired. I was tired of running. Tired of duplicity. Tired of "hanging on." Tired of the way of the world and all the people in it.

Why should I live? What was the point of my life? Where was I going to go? Back to my family identity in Chicago? Back to my identity in abusive relationships, addictions, and self-destruction? Back to my career identity? Back to my identity in my marriage and Mike's family?

Here I am, recently married to the man of my now fractured fairy tale, driving aimlessly on a remote stretch of a canyon road, with despair so deep in my heart that I wanted to end my life. And as remarkable as this sounds, suddenly, peace replaced my hopeless heart in one miraculous moment. In reflection, I believe it was in this experience, where I felt, for the first time in fifty years, God's presence.

My closed and hardened heart opened up to God. This once frowning judge reigning somewhere above the clouds was now my best, and only, friend. God gripped my heart, and in reflection, I believe this is where I met Jesus.

Strange as it sounds, I didn't even know God was present. I didn't get light-headed or begin hallucinating. No harps were playing with angels descending. If God was speaking, his words came softly. His presence was unintelligible.

This experience was unimaginable because I only knew "of" God through the Catholic teaching. My Catholic teachers never taught me it was possible to "know" God through a personal relationship. Further, I resolved years ago that I no longer believed in God or any other higher power, so what was happening to me? Could I be more than randomly firing scientific neurons?

This epiphany awakened my affections for something bigger than myself to a degree I didn't fully understand. Some lessons become apparent only after going a certain distance and reflecting upon the crossroads with more clarity. This supernatural power of the Holy Spirit engulfing my soul and capturing my heart was ethereal and transcendent.

I didn't see anything with my naked eye or hear anything with my ears, but, in a moment, beyond my deepest despair, I felt safe, and I experienced a sense of peace I had never felt before. The eyes of my heart were open to receive the Light of the World.

There has to be a crack to let in the light. A closed and hardened heart cannot receive light. The crosshair on my broken heart's fault line was the crack God's light came in through. The wind of God's

Spirit swept over me. Jesus's light overcame my darkness, and in a single moment, I decided not to end my life. Jesus saved my life.

I don't know how God does what he does. God has a bigger perspective than any human, and he can see what we can't see. God loves each person he made, and he wants us to do all the glorious things he has planned for us.

I don't know why my family of origin and my family through marriage mistreated me, but God always turns terrible to good, never leaving us nor forsaking us. In hindsight, I see this is where God started weaving the mess I had made of my life into the will of his plan. But transforming a five-decade-old worldview into a Christian worldview takes time. I was about to learn the cost of following Jesus.

CHAPTER SIX

PARENTING IDENTITY

I returned home to Mike and my marriage, but I had much to learn about forgiveness to make our relationship right. Mike and I hadn't even reached our first anniversary, and we could feel the distance between us growing. Still, our love for one another proved more durable than our disappointments, and we stayed committed to our marriage.

Despite all this, I was also loyal to my commitment to Mike's mom and remained her primary caregiver for the next eighteen months until she passed away. My mother-in-law and I shared a unique and loving bond for most of our relationship, but we became estranged in her last days for reasons only partially understood.

The strain of the continued rejection from Mike's family proved challenging. During my counseling sessions, my therapist, recognizing my desire to love and nurture, suggested that we adopt a child. Mike and I both had medical issues that prevented us from being biological parents. We didn't research other alternatives since I was fifty to his fifty-five years when we married. We also never considered adoption during the seven years we dated because, precounseling, we assumed Mike's family would support his happiness, thinking his family would welcome anyone who brought him so much joy.

I remember sharing with Mike's daughters, pre- and postcounseling, that I did not intend to be their mother. They were far too old for that relationship, and it wasn't my place, nor ever my intent or desire to have that kind of bond with them. It seemed to me they were more than receptive to my heart's posture.

The way I remember joining Mike's family, I tried my best to be respectful toward his daughters and other family members, encouraging and supporting the relationships they each had with Mike. I recall doing this by making a legacy book for his mom and gifting a copy to each of her siblings, children, and grandchildren.

I remember adorning our home with Mike's many photographs with his daughters and celebrating family birthdays, holidays, and special occasions with generosity and love. I don't remember discouraging any of his family relationships, just the opposite. I recall honoring them in every way I knew how.

But the ongoing sweeping rejection inclined us to open our hearts to adoption. At this point in our lives, it seemed like having a loving family was unattainable through either mine or Mike's family. Still, we desperately wanted to belong to a loving family, so we forged ahead.

The first thing we learned about adoption was that we knew nothing about adoption. We had more misconceptions about the process than we did accurate ones. We thought if our midlife ages didn't hinder our chances of being matched as parents, we would still have to wait years for placement, and adding years to our ages seemed like it would contribute to that obstacle. We also thought, we could not adopt an infant from the US but would instead need to choose an older child overseas.

We learned we were wrong on every account, so in our desire to nurture a child together in a loving family and armed with these new insights, we committed to begin the adoption process. Mindful that we were subjecting a child to a life with older parents, we planned to give the process one year. If it didn't happen within that time, we would withdraw our application, accepting that younger parents would be a better match for an adopted child.

Mike, raised and schooled in the Catholic faith from kindergarten to Jesuit trained college, was a devout Catholic who went to church every Sunday. I didn't go to church with Mike at any point during our dating relationship. However, just after our marriage, when the adoption process began, I returned to church with him because we decided if God blessed us with a child, we would raise our child to know God. In the months during my return to the Catholic Church, I prayed for the child and family I always wanted.

Adoption is more than a journey, and every adoption story is unique. I felt like God heard and answered my prayer because we adopted a child born in a hospital ten miles from our home within one year. We drove the birth mother to the hospital during her labor, and we were by her side as she gave birth to a healthy baby girl. I felt honored to cut the cord of life that attached our daughter to her birth mother. Finally, at long last, I held in my arms the dream that grew in my heart since I was a child, and I became a mom. Had I finally found my true identity in my daughter and purpose through motherhood?

Mike and I didn't want to return to the Catholic Church. Still, we both wanted to raise our baby girl in faith. So, we started by attending a church near our home, where God began shaping my servant heart as I volunteered, first, in a children's ministry and, later, in a counseling ministry.

I taught pre-K through sixth-grade kids how to have a relationship with God, and through this teaching, I learned how to have a relationship with God. While serving children, I felt God also calling me to the church's counseling ministry.

As I sat under the preaching and teaching of Pastor Rick Warren, stirring questions of identity and purpose revealed a new dimension of suffering, which led to a nine-month training program to become a lay Christian counselor for Saddleback Church. God wanted to use my past and pain to repurpose me to share my story of Jesus with other brokenhearted sufferers and survivors.

Mike and I began leading a Bible study in our home with three other married couples. We got baptized at Saddleback Church as our infant daughter looked on from our new spiritual family's arms. We became closer to these six people than our own biological families.

One of the greatest gifts I received from Pastor Rick I learned from his book, *The Purpose Driven Life*.

> "Your spiritual family is even more important than your physical family because it will last forever. Our families on earth are wonderful gifts from God, but they are temporary and fragile, often broken by divorce, distance, growing old, and inevitably, by death but our spiritual family—our relationship to other believers—will continue throughout eternity. It is a much stronger union, a more permanent bond, than blood relationships."
>
> —Rick Warren, *The Purpose Driven Life: What on Earth Am I Here For?* (Grand Rapids: Zondervan, 2002), 120.

Saddleback Church is where I came to faith, and Pastor Rick Warren is someone whose influence bore substantially on my understanding of Christianity. My spiritual family continues to be my most treasured relationships. I realize now that I'm more bound with other believers than anybody else, regardless of their DNA, ethnicity, heritage, culture, color, or language.

Our family of God is so much more important than our family of origin because the family that we were born into, unless believers, is temporary and will perish. But as believers, we will see one another again as God's family in our eternal life.

God was preparing me for a life-changing revelation by showing me why a relationship with Jesus and other believers will always be more enduring and affectionate over any other. I was about to discover my true identity and purpose are not my family, work, marriage, or parenting.

PART TWO

GOD'S STORY

CHAPTER SEVEN

GOD'S STORY

I never knew a memory I wanted to hold, a belief I wanted to own, or a purpose I understood until I met Jesus. He gave me a reason to live and a truth more reliable than any I'd ever known. Like many, I have father hunger. I long for a father who will protect and nurture me, and I want to belong to a family.

To one degree or another, we all suffer. Suffering leaves us with the inescapable agony that we need rescue. We all need a savior. Everything valuable I've learned has come through affliction and not happiness. Jesus said, "Blessed are those who mourn" (Matthew 5:4). He didn't say blessed are those who don't mourn.

Jesus taught me to guard my heart from ruin through a new God-centered identity. I want to share how, through God's preparation, I discovered my identity, tracing God's hand through my suffering, as that which brought me freedom. Pain teaches me that my best response to people who hurt or offend me is to believe that God is in control and know that vengeance belongs to him. More on this follows in subsequent chapters.

The most beautiful story to tell is rooted in truth. I'm a truth seeker. Everything about Jesus rings of truth. Jesus is real. By a miracle of grace, he transformed my life. Some win the battle of suffering, but not all conquer it. We are all soldiers in this battle. Jesus teaches me bitter comes before sweet. He is powerful and pure, giving life like no one I knew before him could.

Growing up, I didn't have role models or mentors. I wanted safety and needed nurture. I wasn't, I don't think, looking for anything necessarily sacred, but along came the most Holy of Holies who transformed my heart and saved my soul.

God chose me, and he loves me radically and unconditionally like no one before ever could, or ever can, love me. One of the most beautiful gifts from Jesus is that he teaches me to accept and understand, not ignore, pain. The world and other people taught me, mostly through self-righteous judgment, to bury, turn a blind eye, and think happy thoughts—do anything, they said, but never reveal my past and pain.

Many people don't know how to remember. Some hold so tightly to their pasts that they can't let go. And if they're holding on to memories with unforgiving hearts, they will toil in bitter resentment the rest of their lives and never be free from their bondage to it. Some live so far in the future that they're paralyzed with fear because the weight of trying to control everything is more than they can hold.

Others live so much in the present that they ignore both the past and the future and busy themselves with distractions to avoid the pain of recalling old wounds or new possibilities. The busyness that they *think* makes them present only distracts them from being truly present. When I reflect on the past, present, and future, living within the healthy tension of balancing all three, I experience freedom from trivial life pursuits.

Jesus teaches me that if I cover up my former life because the memories are too painful or shameful, I will never reach my full potential. The past reminds me of where I came from and of who I am. If I only study the simple parts of a subject and skip learning the hard-to-learn parts, I won't get the highest possible score. I will never grow.

I need to remember what God has done for me and promised to me, so I read the Bible to remember. In turn, God remembers me. It's as if he deconstructs me limb by limb to remake or "re-member" me to reconnect the broken pieces to the real source of light and power—Jesus—and to the people he places in my life. Jesus is the never-ending fountain of all-satisfying water. He is the way, the truth, and the life (John 14:6).

Living in the present with an intentional focus on my relationships, and not with busyness and distractions, grounds me in reality. And thinking about the future gives me hope as a Christian. I know where I'm going. I have a goal, so when the going gets tough, and I hit the rough patches in life, I focus on what matters most.

None of us are untouched by reality and the temporary trappings of what others tell us measure happiness and success. Happiness is fleeting, accomplishments come and go, and success is short-lived. Jesus taught me to hold lightly what I value greatly because it is not mine anyway. There is a day coming when the cause of all my works on earth will be complete. My struggle must be part of the ultimate conclusion. We enjoy the world for a season, but the soul continues forever.

In the remaining chapters, you will see how God's Story brings clarity to life's meaning and how that bridges to our collective story as adopted children in the family of God. The following chapters provide scriptural wisdom and personal insights to help you answer:

1. Who am I?
2. What's the point of my life?
3. How do I have healthy relationships?
4. How do I forgive the unforgivable?
5. How do I live a lasting legacy?

God's Story helps you understand how your identity, purpose, relationships, forgiveness, and legacy show that the meaning of life is to connect and reflect God. Discovering my identity and the meaning of life through a relationship with Jesus happened when I surrendered my desire for control, and my heart opened to his teachings.

In the remaining chapters, you will see how to:

1. Embrace identity through truth
2. Discover purpose through obedience
3. Grow relationships through love

4. Experience forgiveness through humility
5. Live legacy through faith

God is the ultimate source of truth, wisdom, and joy. My prayer is that God opens your heart's eyes to consider these insights and reveals the freedom that comes from L.I.G.H.T. (Living in God's Holy Truth).

CHAPTER EIGHT

IDENTITY IN CHRIST

Natural Birth

I believe people want to be kind and loving toward others, but we are unable to without the saving grace and love of Jesus because we are all born with sin in our hearts. As I began studying the Bible, I saw who I am through God's truth, but first, I had to recognize and admit that I am a sinner with a corrupt heart.

Sinful and corrupt are harsh words often taken with great offense. I remember the first time someone told me I was "sinful" with a "corrupt and rebellious hard heart." I was deeply hurt but mostly confused, thinking the sinner label applied to murderers and rapists or hard-core criminals. I thought I didn't belong to these people groups. But how wrong I was.

We learn from the Bible that God appointed Adam to represent humanity; every one of us come from Adam, the father of humanity. The first command in the Bible is in Genesis: "And the LORD God commanded the man, saying, 'You may surely eat of every tree of the garden, but of the tree of the knowledge of good and evil you shall not eat, for in the day that you eat of it you shall surely die'" (Genesis 2:16–17).

When Adam ate the forbidden fruit and sinned, that sin became our sin, as did God's judgment. So when Adam failed, we failed too. When Adam fell into sin ("the fall"), it forever altered human nature. Adam, along with all of us, became estranged from God. Every person on earth is born with hostility against God and a corrupt heart, which leads us to sin from an early age.

We make our own choices because we think we know what is best for us. Sin is choosing to treasure anything over God. If we're left to decide what's right and wrong, there's no end to our rationalization of good and evil. We all need God's wisdom to discern what is good and evil. "For my people have committed two evils: they have forsaken me, the fountain of living waters, and hewed out cisterns for themselves, broken cisterns that can hold no water" (Jeremiah 2:13).

Acknowledging we are all born into sin-motivated rebellion sounds utterly hopeless. Still, we are not without hope because, generations after the fall, God sent his Son, Jesus, to stand in Adam's place as a kind of second Adam, or "last Adam" (1 Corinthians 15:45). Jesus came to save all of us who desperately need a savior. In one extraordinary life and astonishing death of obedience, Jesus undid what Adam did. When Jesus rose from the dead, new creation, or new life, began. Jesus obeyed where Adam failed. God gave us a way to conquer sin and death and hell, but, he said, we must be born again to receive it (John 3:3).

Jesus lived a sinless life. He died for our sins and endured God's wrath, paying the penalty for our sins that we should have suffered because they are our sins, not his. Jesus bought us eternal life with his blood and secured the promises of God for all of us. He rose from the dead, conquering death and hell and Satan. Jesus intervened for us, and he will come again.

Jesus uses harsh words like "corrupt" and "sinful," to show us hard truths about ourselves and the world. I didn't agree that I was a rebellious, hard-hearted sinner when I first heard it, but it doesn't change the reality that I am naturally a rebellious, hard-hearted sinner. Only when I accepted Jesus, supernaturally, did my heart change. He transformed me from the inside out through a new birth.

I have since come to cherish and savor Jesus's truth, all of it—the easy and the hard truths. Admittedly, owning my sin still hurts, but swallowing those hard truth pills is easier because I understand my nature more clearly after finding my identity in Christ.

Sometime after the adoption process began, I asked my mother-in-law if she thought I would make a good mom. She said, "Yes." She was a woman of few words. I had to ask more if I wanted more. So, I asked her why she thought I would be a good mom. "Because," my mother-in-law said, "you have suffered much." She was right. I have suffered much. I don't know if past suffering helps in parenting, but I believe my pain has made me appreciate truth—to the extent that "I am a truth seeker" became my battle cry. Why do I seek the truth, you might ask? Because, quite simply, truth brings freedom.

There may be few contemporary movie one-liners more memorable than Jack Nicholson's from the 1992 military courtroom drama *A Few Good Men*. In the last act, Nicholson, who plays a decorated Colonel with an illustrious career and the potential to one day receive a general's star, testifies in a murder trial after a Marine in his command died during a hazing incident. Many consider the two-minute tirade to defend his honor a masterpiece as he concludes with the iconic line, "You can't handle the truth." It was almost impossible for me not to get swept up in the "Oorah" of this drama. In part because Nicholson's portrayal of the tough and unforgiving military life was so superb, but more so because it resonated deeply with me as I contrasted his life to mine.

I lost count of how many times I watched that movie. "You can't handle the truth" was carved in my heart and worn like a badge of honor. Deep inside, I, too, had a hard heart. Living in a world where only the strong survive and shouldering a disproportionate burden of suffering that others did not, I felt self-righteous in my anger over my misfortunes and lost opportunities. When people whimpered about little things, my pride swelled because I was confident that they could never handle the truth.

How could they ever know what actual pain was? They couldn't understand what suffering was because they want other people's lives to get messy and burdened with trouble so they can deny the hard truths about their lives and be clean and comfortable in their pain-free lives.

I clung to that truth mantra until the day Jesus reoriented my affections for his truth statement, "You will know the truth, and the truth will set you free" (John 8:32). I can't tell you how Jesus transformed my heart of stone, but I can tell you when and where it happened. It was 2010, contemplating suicide in the quiet of a car on a remote canyon road in Southern California. Because of that supernatural transformation, I no longer carry the weight of past or future suffering.

Before that miracle, I was sinking into a bottomless abyss, living a delusional life, losing my ability to accept hard truth and reality, pursuing my happiness through a cycle of insignificant fleeting pleasures. I was blind to harsh realities because it was too difficult to face the truth. I hid the truth until Jesus showed me a better way. Life is sometimes cruel, but Jesus showed me running from that reality wasn't helping my situation or changing the truth. Jesus teaches humility and shows me how to swallow my pride and accept the truth rather than shifting blame in my fight-or-flight responses. This heart transformation allows me to experience more joy and peace.

I used to let earthly relationships, possessions, achievements, and failures define me, attaching my identity to my family, drinking, work, and marriage. But God designed us to look up to him for our identity, not left and right or toward other people and materialism. In loving and imitating other people and things in the world that God created rather than God himself, I was permitting other idols to define me, which only leads to disappointment, insecurity, and confusion.

We're all, in some measure, influenced by worldly people who try to form our identities. With my natural self-centered worldview, I always felt pressured to fit into a nonspiritual mold. Though I came to faith just after becoming a mom, it still took time to learn this false idol principle.

Having no success with family, drinking, work, and marriage, I attempted to find my identity through my daughter, boasting about her exceptional character and achievements that, even as a baby, were so clear. I thought I deserved the parent-of-the-year award when she accomplished something extraordinary. In reality, God was gradually revealing to me it's never about anything I do. It's always about what God does.

God created us—body, mind, and soul. We owe every morsel of strength we have to God, every seed of intelligence to him, and the slightest act of love or kindness we express is a gift from him. Our abilities, too, are good gifts from God. Apart from God's grace, we're helpless.

Mike and I raise our daughter in a God-centered, truth-based home, she attends a Christian school and church, but that doesn't guarantee she will not stray from her faith. There will come a day when my daughter, like everyone else, must choose to surrender her life to God or to grasp for control. Only God knows if, like the Prodigal Son, her appetite for virtue may, one day, fade (perhaps when she enters the broader secular culture) and cause her to walk away from her faith. Mindful of Jesus's teaching "in the world but not of the world," we try to prepare her for worldly temptation, but we may lose or gain our daughter either way (1 John 2:15). We cannot bear the weight of her, or anyone else's, destiny. That's God's authority.

Finding my identity in relationships will never work because we are all broken humans living in a fallen world, and our lives are temporary. We will all die. When I expect someone other than God to define me, inevitably, through sin (mine or the other persons) or death, I will experience disappointment. The teachings of Jesus are so contrary to the self-centered, "it's all about me," and "have it your way" narcissistic mindset that I once had.

Learning my true identity was a hard-fought battle, but God never gave up his pursuit to teach me what matters most in knowing who I am. God went deeper to show me why my love for my daughter was so intense, revealing that I had such an unconditionally radical love for my daughter because I needed so much. I was trying to heal wounds from the lack of love, acceptance, and nurture I never received, which I thought every child wanted and needed.

I thought all I had to do was love my child, and she would respond with love and gratitude. That was and is not the case. My daughter is a person in her own right with gifts, desires, and needs separate from mine. The lessons God teaches me about my pride and self-centeredness are endless.

One of the most distinguishing marks of a Christian is God-centeredness. Following Jesus teaches me not to see my identity in self-centeredness. My identity is outside of myself in God. God is my power, and he gives me life and strength to live it. As an image-bearer of Christ, created in God's image, my life reflects his. I root my identity in my understanding that God created me in his image and sent his Son, Jesus, to suffer and die for my sins so I could be born again with fresh life, ultimately receiving eternal life (Genesis 1:27; 2:7; John 3:16).

Spiritual Birth

Baptized at Saddleback Church with my husband, Mike, I became a committed Jesus follower through a new spiritual birth. Spiritual birth is a creation of a new human nature, forgiven, cleansed, and formed from the inside out, through God's Spirit indwelling in me. In my rebirth, the Holy Spirit united me in a living union with God. God is the vine where life flows, and we are the branches (John 15:1–11).

In my new birth, my old self died in the light of my faith in Jesus, and I rose in freedom. The warrior, workhorse, self-centered, prideful me died and rose in freedom. My freedom comes from knowing, even though I will never walk in sinless perfection, that's not the goal—my goal is to trust God, I can still rise above my sin and be free from the bondage to it.

I now see *original* sin as a universal condition, due to Adam's sin that mysteriously passes down to all (Romans 5:12–19). But sin is also a choice we make, as we mature. And we are all guilty of both—sinners by birthright and sinners by choice. I hate sin the way God hates it, and I confess it. When I confess my sin and accept Jesus, my heart awakens to the beauty of God. This instantaneous awakening that simultaneously produces my faith in Jesus is what the Bible calls justification. With justification, a progressive transformation to improve my morally ruined character begins. This transformation, that the Bible calls sanctification, continues throughout life.

In our new birth, God pours his Holy Spirit into our souls, and his Spirit now dwells in us to help us live in obedience to God's greatest commandment, which is to love God, love others, and love ourselves. As God's image-bearers, we continue transformation by the daily renewing of our minds in our obedience to walk with God (Romans 12:2)

All of God's commands to love or obey are calling me to be like him. I respect his call for my obedience, knowing I will never be perfect in my earthly life but striving to be as Christlike as possible. Every day dawns for me with the breath of life—all by God's providence to keep me. God knew the day I would be born, and he knows the day I will die when he calls me to my eternal home in heaven with him.

> And we all, with unveiled face, beholding the glory of the Lord, are being transformed into the same image from one degree of glory to another. For this comes from the Lord who is the Spirit. (2 Corinthians 3:18)

When Adam sinned, he fell spiritually, and his spirit became estranged from God. Our separation from God yearns to get back to the place Adam once enjoyed before the fall. There is a spiritual hunger inside all of us to reconcile to a perfect relationship with God.

I didn't recognize that my heart longed to know and be with God. This hunger drove me to worldly things to satisfy that internal craving. Longing for God drives all of us, in our ignorance, to seek pleasure and material things to fulfill our needs. Those material things or people we prefer over God become false idols in our hearts.

To understand my true identity required humbling myself to admit that my security, individuality, and significance come from outside myself, from God. I replaced my self-centeredness with God-centeredness and my self-esteem with God-esteem and found my true identity.

The dictionary defines identity as: "the distinguishing character or personality of an individual." What is my distinguishing character or personality? Some people, myself included, look to psychology for answers to help them understand their personalities. Contemporary psychology looks toward positive aspects of human nature, virtue, and the importance of gratitude, forgiveness, and altruism. Lest we forget, humans have fallen, and sin has stained God's image in all of us. We're all capable of evil and sin. That's why we all need Jesus.

God created us as spiritual beings with order and balance, but even though we're all made in God's image, we have unique traits. Simple observations of newborn babies prove that we're born different. Some babies laugh a lot, and some do not. Some love closeness and swaddling, while others do not. Babies are already unique at birth. Many people carry hidden resentment toward God for not creating them how they would have designed themselves, but it's foolish to think we're wiser than God. David wrote:

> For you formed my inward parts;
>   you knitted me together in my mother's womb.
> I praise you, for I am fearfully and wonderfully made.
>   Wonderful are your works;
>   my soul knows it very well.
> My frame was not hidden from you,
> when I was being made in secret,
>   intricately woven in the depths of the earth.
> Your eyes saw my unformed substance; in your book
> were written, every one of them,
>   the days that were formed for me,
>   when as yet there was none of them.
>   (Psalm 139:13–16)

Through divine inspiration, David knew that before we were born, God designed us. While God differentiated our bodies within our mothers' wombs, each inward part was intentional, including our strengths and weaknesses.

I believe God created us with different strengths and weaknesses to accomplish all there is to do in the kingdom of God. We cannot have every possible Christlike character, but we can have attributes that individually contribute to the body of work needed in God's kingdom.

It seems God uses various things to affect our uniqueness, from genetics, birth order, temperament, physicality, health, and other people he places in our lives. Regardless of what we call it, we all have something that makes us different in our attitudes and behaviors from others, but precisely what that is, we cannot fully understand this side of eternity. What's important to understand is that our identities remain intact. We are who we are because God is who God is. We root our identities in Christ.

As God was slowly revealing this truth to me, I reflected on how the first half of my life mirrored my dad's life. Despite my dad's drinking, he appeared sober because he was a hard worker and achieved career success, often boasting how he never missed work. His strong work ethic made it easy for him to deny his alcoholism and justify frequent social cocktail gatherings. It was only later in his life that he stopped drinking when doctors discovered a health problem.

I also achieved career success, denying that I had a drinking problem because of my tolerance to an increasing consumption. My life started spinning out of control when I began overindulging in social circles, not realizing I had more than I could handle. My blackouts and hangovers served as a cruel reminder that my drinking was no longer a naughty habit. It was an addiction decaying by the day. Fortunately, I did not stop because of a health diagnosis; I stopped because of a heart transformation.

My heartache had no cure until I met Jesus. Jesus diagnosed my heart as the root of my problem—my heart was an enchanted prison. Prison because I lived in bondage to things I treasured more than God and enslaved to my sin and enchanted because my sins were so sweet to my flesh. And it was here, inside my heartland battleground, where I the warrior fought these sins every day.

It wasn't long after my encounter with Jesus when I came home from work one evening and, not unlike most evenings, reached for a bottle of wine to help me relax after a busy day. I didn't know then why this happened, but I let it go as soon as I reached for the bottle.

Shortly after that, I was celebrating Mike's birthday and enjoying cocktails when suddenly, after thirty years, I set my empty glass of wine on the table and never had another drink again. It wasn't a deliberate decision to stop drinking. That was, at present-day writing, ten years ago.

It was also around this time that I stopped working in the corporate world so I could be a stay-at-home mom, and oddly enough, it was also during this time that I stopped watching television. I would later learn why I made all of those random and unconscious choices.

Work had become my safe haven; the only place I got accolades and positive reinforcement. Inheriting my dad's strong work ethic, I had been coming home to relax on my couch and defaulting to wine and TV each day after work. It had started with celebrity entertainment, followed by whatever the latest popular show was. Admiring and idolizing celebrities, I had tried to be like them. I had followed their beauty tips and bought the clothes they wore to imitate them. I had been so image-conscious that celebrity stars appealed to me. And I had been so status-conscious that my career was my top priority. My job had become my identity.

My self-consciousness had been crippling and all-consuming. I had been living by what the world taught me was important: me. I was the sole focus of my life. It was all about me. How good I could look. How much money I could earn. What neighborhood I could live in and what kind of car I could drive. What vacations I could take, who I could hang out with, and what parties I could attend. And on and on.

I was living in Beverly Hills, California, earning a six-figure income during this time. I remember feeling impressed with myself and proud of my accomplishments because of where I had come from and because I was "uneducated," at least from a worldly perspective. Because my formative years didn't provide the opportunities for a formal, degreed education, I always had to work a little harder to get noticed and to achieve success. Enter ninja workhorse. The management positions I held resulted from starting at the bottom to prove myself while keeping my nose to the grindstone and clearing inboxes to work my way up.

These were not peripheral issues; instead, this had been my epiphany of the true meaning of life. God revealed that my pride—being the major actor and enormous star of my life—was my sin. Sin was the issue. And it's everybody's issue because it's a universal condition. Whether the sin involves sex and adultery; desiring wealth, power, position or prestige; drunkenness; drugs; dishonesty; narcissism; gossip; or unbelief, we are all sinners. I was powerless to the weight of sin and imprisoned to it until I realized that even though I was born with a sinful nature, I still had free will to chose it or not. What does this say about our souls' depravity that we enjoy these pleasures over and above God?

I chose pride, arrogance, selfishness, alcohol, and entertainment over God. My pleasures knew no boundaries with the idols of my heart. It appalled me to learn how shallow and self-centered I was, but the revelation that changed my life was the understanding that the root cause of all of it was, and is, my sin. By birthright, from the father of humanity, the first Adam, I am a sinner. And underneath all this, my biggest sin was not choosing God first. I was so in love with myself that I felt entitled to my pleasures and privileges. I became indignant when I didn't get my way.

Worldly, not godly, people tried to teach me to find my identity in relationships. The media encouraged me to live vicariously through celebrities and famous people who flaunt their images through entertainment and social media platforms, only to gain popularity. I see now what silly nonsense it is that people I didn't even know could impress me. And I also now see how insecure I was to want to imitate someone who doesn't even know, let alone care about me.

God knows us intimately like a parent knows their child. God's continuous devotion to us establishes our identities as his children. He remembers us when we mess up and loves us unconditionally, despite our mistakes. We are chosen, created through birth and rebirth, and known by God. From dust to man, we are in God's image. Our faith in Jesus secures our identities in God on earth and in eternity. From womb to tomb, God is our identity.

For years I wrestled with questions about the meaning of life. Frustrated with the empty promises of selfhood, I needed to understand the significance of my life. And only when God gave me a new identity through rebirth did my life made sense. I finally realized who I was and why I was born, but I needed to be born again for it to make sense.

Receiving new spiritual birth from a supernatural, transcendent being pushes the limits of the human mind. I was trying to comprehend and control a reality that defies language and intellect. Once that stronghold broke loose, and I opened my narrow-minded and self-centered thinking, I saw that my true identity is in God. I surrendered my pride and the need to control my life. I stopped living for myself and started living for God.

Jesus won my affections, causing me to desire him more than the sin in my heart. When I opened my heart to believe in Christ, I freed myself from the bondage of sin and the guilt of my misdirected desires and choices. My battle was recognizing my willpower could not conquer my sinful external behaviors. I needed God to severe the root of my sinful passions to incline my heart to desire him more. Opening our hearts to God is the mark of our rebirth as Christians, and one of our highest spiritual disciplines is to allow God to change our sinful desires into godly desires.

May God grant you eyes to see, ears to hear, and a heart to understand his teaching. "Truly, truly, I say to you, unless one is born again he cannot see the kingdom of God" (John 3:3). My prayer is that God will awaken your soul and quicken your affections toward the Christian life to understand that your true identity is in God. What I learned next is how crucial understanding my identity is in discerning the meaning of life.

CHAPTER NINE

PURPOSE IN CHRIST

God-Centered

Once I understood my identity in Christ, I needed to know why God made me. The Bible teaches us that God made us for his glory (Isaiah 43:7). We know this is true because it's written in God's Word, and all Scripture is God-breathed (John 17:17; 2 Timothy 3:16–17).

God created us to reflect to the world who he is so he can look great in making and saving us. When we do this, others see that our love and joy comes from him. Some people hear this and think God is an egomaniac; they don't understand how this can be love. What kind of person, they say, would create something only to glorify themselves? In reality, it's the other way around.

God knows he is our supreme significance. As we have seen, no other person, physical pleasure, or material comfort of this world will ever be enough to satisfy our deepest desires. God created us so we can know him and delight in him because what he gives us is better than anything else we will receive. Nobody can give what God gives.

So, it's a loving God who sacrifices his perfect and sinless Son to die for our sins, freely giving us the greatest love and joy that we can ever experience. The love God gives us brings us enduring joy. And that joy is in knowing, admiring, and reflecting the most beautiful person in the universe Jesus Christ, who is God.

Jesus does for us what we could never do for ourselves. A person whose only concern was for himself would not do this. Would you sacrifice your life through an inhumane crucifixion only to bear the punishment for the entire world's sins and then freely give eternal life to every sinner? Who, other than a loving and sacrificial God, would do that?

Our purpose is to connect and reflect God. We connect with God through our relationship with him, and we reflect God by loving him and serving others. Reflecting and loving God and serving others satisfies our longing for significance and honors God when others see him in us. One effect of my rebirth is confidence and trust that the abundance of God's love and grace in me will overflow to others.

Connection with God happened for me as I developed a personal relationship with him through prayer (talking to God) and reading the Bible (hearing his truth). Reflection of God happens in my obedience to follow him, which I do when I serve others with my time and spiritual gifts. We're each called to serve others cheerfully, without grumbling or a spirit of obligation to merit God's favor. We serve others with the gifts that God has freely given us. In my rebirth, I died to my former self-serving life, giving rise to a new life of serving others. I could only do this by opening my heart to God and renewing my mind.

God transforms me into a new, right relationship with him and others, which reorients my hardened heart of self-centeredness to place others' needs before my own. God's light called me out of darkness through new birth to enjoy my identity in Christ and live the way God originally designed it to be in the garden of Eden before the fall.

I am right with God because of my faith in him. Now I get the incredible privilege to reflect him and his love (God is love!) through loving and worshiping him and loving and serving others, so I can stop looking to false idols to satisfy my desires. Loving and honoring

God and serving others progresses throughout my life as I become, through my life experiences, who I am in Christ by living in obedience to him.

Jesus paid the price for my sins with his blood. If I accept that, I should act like it. My yes should be a yes, and my no should be a no. Do I accept that Jesus died for my sins? Yes, I do. So, my old self dies, and now I'm in a right (new) relationship with God (through justification by faith), living my life in obedience to him. God commands my obedience, but I cannot do that in my strength, so I accept Jesus's help, letting the Holy Spirit transform my mind and my will (Philippians 2:13).

Others-Centered

The Bible teaches me to consider others above myself: "Do nothing from selfish ambition or conceit but in humility count others more significant than yourselves" (Philippians 2:3). When I love God and serve others, I become S.A.L.T. (Serving and Loving Together) and L.I.G.H.T. (Living in God's Holy Truth). Serving and loving together, living in God's holy truth, honors God because I reflect his life in mine when I do that.

We have seen that the Holy Spirit gives us new spiritual life in our connection to Jesus through our faith. The Bible teaches that when this happens, our souls shape into the people who love to do the will of God (Ezekiel 36:27).

Our souls are not transforming under duress. The Holy Spirit molds us from the inside out, so we believe that virtuous acts, like being kind to others, or finding beauty in truth, or serving others rather than serving our own needs, are the most rewarding things we can do in life.

Let me explain how transformation worked in my life. Shortly after coming to faith, I gradually began eliminating false idols (sin) from my life. I didn't understand this at the time when I stopped drinking, or when I chose not to care about celebrity-saturated media, or when I realized the sitcom sewer of secular TV and entertainment was actually really distasteful, or that my identity was, in fact, not my family, drinking, career, marriage, or daughter. But I see it all so clearly now because God is continually (in stages) renewing my mind through a change of heart and a shift in thinking.

> Do not be conformed to this world, but be transformed by the renewal of your mind, that by testing you may discern what is the will of God, what is good and acceptable and perfect. For by the grace given to me I say to everyone among you not to think of himself more highly than he ought to think, but to think with sober judgment, each according to the measure of faith that God has assigned. (Romans 12:2–3)

Stepping down from my high horse and becoming zealous for a good and holy God, I saw how much I care about the quality of my life's spiritual and moral dimensions. But let's be clear—my goal was not then, and is not now, to become sinless—no one will ever achieve sinless perfection on earth. Instead, I now see my sins in God's light, not my darkness, and I respond to my sinful nature the way God does.

I could tell the supernatural presence of Jesus was real when I saw that the things I loved to do, like following Jesus and showing love and grace to others, was what I ought to do. When you would rather love than hate, or feel contentment over envy, or give rather than receive, or believe it's better to be kind than cruel, or humble yourself to forgive someone who hurt you—when any of these things happen in you, then you know that you are born again.

It's a miracle when you awaken to such affections because you see that God is in you, forming your soul from the inside out to regenerate a new, cleansed, forgiven (not sinless) nature. I experienced the miraculous life of Jesus in me. When faith in Jesus awakened in my heart, I didn't want to love anything or anyone more than God. Jesus became, and remains, first, above all else, in my life.

Jesus lived to honor his Father's will. We need to let Jesus help us be more about God's will. One way we do this is by serving one another, side by side, in unity. Obedience to God grows throughout our lives. When we're obedient to Jesus's calling for us to live humble lives of service toward others, we find purpose. I used to confuse my service to others as a service to Jesus. But then I realized Jesus doesn't need my rescue; it's the other way around.

The Bible awakens our hearts with an extraordinary story about sacrificial love. Jesus taught those closest to him that he came to earth to serve and give, showing them how to live their lives loving and serving others by teaching them to put others' needs above their own.

On the night of his betrayal, Jesus sat with his disciples at the Last Supper. He knew his last hours were upon him, and soon he would hang crucified on a cross, bearing the weight of guilt, suffering for a world of sins he did not commit. And what does Jesus do, knowing he has one last chance to impart wisdom to his disciples? Taking a basin of water, Jesus gets on his hands and knees to wash his disciples' feet, including his betrayer, Judas.

Jesus knew Judas was a traitor, yet he washed his feet. Jesus's attention was on the needs of others. He knew his disciples needed his help. They needed wisdom to understand and strength to endure the horror about to unfold in the hours ahead, and they needed hope to press on and fulfill their purpose without him.

If I believe Jesus died for my sins to make me right with God, then I need to obey his teaching. Some people think since Jesus died for our sins and forgave us, it doesn't matter if we (intentionally or otherwise) mess up because Jesus knows we're sinners, and he's already forgiven us. That is not biblical.

The Bible does not say that we can continue in sin because Jesus bought us with his blood. We have work to do as Christians in obeying God's commands. But it will cost us, just as it cost Jesus his life. As he prayed in Luke, "Father, if you are willing, remove this cup from me. Nevertheless, not my will, but yours, be done" (Luke 22:42).

We suffer, sacrifice, and pay the price in our obedience to be like Jesus. So count the cost before becoming a Christian. But, take heart, because Jesus has overcome the world: "I have said these things to you, that in me you may have peace. In this world you will have tribulation. But take heart; I have overcome the world" (John 16:33).

God commands our obedience, but we can't be or do what we know we're supposed to in our strength, so we look to Jesus. Jesus came to fix what's broken in us. He wants to serve us. He didn't come for us to serve him: "For even the Son of Man came not to be served but to serve, and to give his life as a ransom for many" (Mark 10:45).

Jesus serves us by carrying our burdens giving us his power to be obedient to him. Jesus serves us and gives us his ability to help us live out our purpose in obedience. Jesus gave me his Holy Spirit at my rebirth to renew my mind so that everything I think, feel, and do now shows that God is more valuable than anything else. I don't serve Jesus. Jesus serves me in his strength, and I serve others with the help Jesus gives me (John 14:15–17, 25–26).

Christian servanthood happens only in God's strength, so everything a person does in serving others gets magnified through Jesus. God's power in my service to others brings me joy. I love helping others through God's strength and the gifts he gives me.

Self-Centered

People who don't follow Jesus boast that their strength, intelligence, education, money, power—you fill in the blank—is why they have what they have. When we want control over our lives only to show the world how great we are and use that power over others who are less fortunate than us, then we surrender our real potential to find joy in God and display his greatness.

I know many upwardly mobile people who have job security, a marriage with kids, good health, and financial success who think they achieved these things. They did not. God did. Everything we are, physically and mentally, and everything we have, including our jobs, relationships, and wealth, are God's gifts. When I turned from my self-exalting pride to God-honoring humility, I gained God's power to serve others. I took all that God gave me in gifts and experience and applied it to honor him through lowly and sacrificial servanthood. To the extent possible, I live free of the obsession with false idols and focus on pouring out my life experiences and God's gifts to relieve suffering for others.

Four years after coming to faith and after serving as a children's teacher and Christian counselor at Saddleback Church, Mike, my daughter, and I moved to the East Coast. To say that I didn't want to leave our church or spiritual family in California is an understatement. I did my best to postpone our move by volunteering an additional year as a children's teacher and counselor, but alas, we had to go. So in 2014, covered in God's grace and bathed in prayer from our spiritual family, we followed God's call and moved.

The East Coast church and social culture proved a stark contrast to the West Coast. We faced many challenges that didn't seem to warrant the struggle, such as finding the right church and school for my daughter and meeting neighbors and friends. We pondered how every straightforward transition issue had to be a complicated drama. Repeatedly, I questioned why God sent us to such an awful place. No answer came. I persevered in prayer and pressed on, confident God would reveal it in his time.

It didn't take long until I realized that I was in an unfamiliar world called Small Town America, surrounded by mean-girl cliques. These tribal behaviors where subservient minions did anything to fit in appalled me, but I wanted what was best for my daughter and did what I could to help her find friends. Thinking back to this time, I remember things didn't go well. I'm guessing because I was older than most of the other moms, though upon reflection, I'm sure there were other reasons I didn't make the cut, but to consider the myriad of possibilities exhausts me.

I did my best to attend the required functions at my daughter's preschool until the day I received an email from the group's Queen Bee which she inadvertently sent me in a "reply to all" communication. In the email, she described me in less than flattering ways, displaying all the ugliness that can come via backstabbing pettiness. And though it hurt, I think I was more shocked thinking, "Who, at this age, does this?"

So I was "fired" from the social clique. Having read the Bible and gone far enough in my walk with Jesus, I knew what God was calling me to do. I found an opportunity to confront my adversary, to work it out. We could not reconcile, so I went to another person involved to share my concerns. There was not a happy ending there either. Eventually, I took my daughter out of that school and moved on, only to discover more equally unpleasant encounters in our season of transition.

It wasn't clear why we moved for several months, but what was clear was how God gifted me uniquely to fulfill his purpose. Jesus was, yet again, revealing something more beautiful than I was seeing. Comparing what others had that I didn't and competing with their values to prove my morals better, I was trying to change myself just to fit in.

God's Will

God wanted me to look around, exactly where I was because he was speaking to me in the ordinary and mundane parts of my life to show me his extraordinary grace. Why should I feel slighted being ousted from a clique, and why should it matter if I didn't "fit in" to a particular culture?

God wanted me to change my expectations and stop trying to control my idea of what my life should be (my will). He wanted me to connect to my purpose (his will). Unharmed, I moved on, focusing on the only thing that truly matters—God.

By God's grace, Mike and I both have spirits of radical generosity and hospitality. Shifting our focus and fixing our eyes on Jesus, we began supporting and serving—in financially and nonmonetary ways—other people and various ministries. We opened our home to host regular church community groups and traveling international missionaries who needed a place to stay. We invited one family who had a house fire to live with us during their transition. In 2018 we purchased property to launch a Christian nonprofit called the Family Peace Center, where we help families build healthy relationships with God and others. Using God's gifts of our collective corporate (seventy years) and ministry (twenty years) experiences, in big and small ways, Mike and I now dedicate our time, talent, and finances to share the overflow of God's love and gifts in our lives with others.

We want to share the reality of God's work in our lives with other families who struggle with similar challenges in their lives because we believe to find peace and purpose in your life, you must begin with God. We see our life purpose through our faith in Jesus and our obedience to him in our service to others.

The Christian counseling certification that I received in California was only valid for my counseling through the Saddleback Church ministry, so I pursued a nationally recognized accreditation to serve our new nonprofit counseling ministry. After completing a four-year distance learning program, I became a Christian counselor and ordained minister of pastoral care.

At the Family Peace Center, we offer youth programs, counseling programs, and development programs. Each ministry of the Family Peace Center focuses on building healthy relationships with a "Be R.E.A.L." mindset. We teach people how to be Respectful, Encouraging, Accepting, and Loving to others with their words and actions.

Respectful, encouraging, accepting, and loving people were missing in my previous life, and I fought hard to find those qualities in others. It's beautiful that I can now give back to others something I never had. Our counseling ministry offers biblical counseling. Our development programs provide support in marriage, parenting, relationships, forgiveness, legacy, identity, purpose, and spiritual growth through a series of "L.I.G.H.T." books and training material. This book is the second publication I have authored in that series.

As a Christian counselor, I comfort and pray for lost souls through God's love. In our youth group, I teach kids how much Jesus loves them. In our development program ministry, I write about Jesus through the brokenness of my life to help people learn to love better. Gifts are not for a few, but for all. We all receive gifts from God that we can use to strengthen each other (1 Peter 4:10–11).

God inspires me to want to be a sage—someone who people want to listen to so they can learn about God's truth; someone who can give a testimony about what it means to walk through darkness and survive affliction—because I have a God who chose me, and set me apart as holy, and loves me like no other.

God had to break my heart to make my heart, but he never left me. God was and is always with me through every storm. Even when I suffered in my former life when I didn't know God, God was with me. I remember barely surviving a few domestically violent nights, but God pulled me through. Moses didn't think he had what he needed to lead his people out of Egypt, but God told him, "I will be with your mouth and teach you what you shall speak" (Exodus 4:12). I think this applies to all of us. God gives us everything we need to shine his light.

Shining God's light in my life starts with renewing my mind with the Word of God. I let his truth seep deep into my soul, so my heart continues to transform to his will. How this happens mystifies me, but I believe in the infinitely complex mind and will of God. I trust that he will give me what I need to accomplish his will.

When I contrast my current life of God-centeredness to my former self-centeredness, I see that this is a rhythm we are all meant to live. There is so much more joy in giving than receiving. As long as I was selfish, I could not be successful.

I know many people who think the meaning of life is about material wealth. Sure, you can become rich in money, but you will never be rich in character if that is your life goal. And you will never make enough because every promotion or increase only leaves you striving for more. I don't want to be puddle shallow; I want to be ocean deep.

Living sacrificially and generously is rewarding. My gifts may look small, but I trust in God's abundance and know that it honors him even in my imperfect achievements because I'm fulfilling my purpose through obedience. And when I fail, I know God has allowed that failure to teach me something. The lesson could be as simple as knowing his desire to draw me closer to himself.

I can't always know why I don't get my way, why God doesn't answer my every prayer, or why I sometimes have upsetting days when things don't turn out the way I planned. I have faced a million and one disappointments in my life and plenty more ahead to experience. I try to accept what comes my way with gratitude and joy. I no longer need instant gratification or validation, nor do I measure success by lack of failure. On the contrary, if I have failed, I have succeeded. For when I am weak, then I am strong (2 Corinthians 12:9–10).

Purpose in Pain

Athletes train to compete and to win. They stretch, press, lift, pump, and run to prepare for the victory. They're off at race pace, working as hard as they can to get to the end. They start strong but eventually fatigue until they grow weary and want to give up.

I do this when I swim. When I'm nearing my last lap, I'm worn out and have nothing left to give. I'm convinced that, if I continue with one more stroke, it will be my last. So I'm tempted to just give up. And it's at that moment, when I want to give up, that God is testing me. He does this to prepare me for the challenges I will inevitably face, because I will have trouble in this life.

Everything in my life built up to my encounter with Jesus. It was the moment in my car, when I wanted to end my life, and I didn't think I could go on. The defeats were too many, and I could only see gathering darkness. The fatal feeling was creeping in. Life wasn't worth it. But that was the moment of most significant impact—the biggest battle that God was preparing me to conquer—not with my strength, but with his power.

Even after praying in that confessional booth as a child, for what I thought was my last time, God didn't leave me. He has always been with me, never giving me more than I could handle, pulling me through every storm.

All I went through before my encounter with Jesus was God's preparation, leading me to discover my identity. You don't train for the easy parts. You don't train just so you can relax. And you don't train for the beginning of the race—everyone is motivated and feels energized initially. You practice for the point in the race when you want to throw in the towel. That's what God prepares us for in our trials. So, when we walk through the valley of the shadow of death, we will be victorious because God has prepared us through testing us. We don't fight for victory. We fight from victory—Jesus's victory—the one he conquered on a hill called Calvary.

There is a dark power in all our lives. That evil power is Satan, the Father of Lies, the Enemy, and his weapon is spiritual warfare. For many, he is a wicked, unwelcome friend, because they haven't learned to lean into the discomfort and pain in their lives and to trust that there is a purpose in their pain and that God will pull them through.

It's in these moments when I feel I can't stand another moment that I need Jesus and my faith the most. I need to trust that God is working all of it together for better purposes. The experiences of our lives frame God's will. When I trust God's will, he revives my soul and renews my strength to endure the trial.

Many people end relationships when it gets complicated. Delete, dispose, and it's over, I'm done with you. Their obedience falters; they don't have faith in God to trust his lead, that there is a higher purpose in their pain. That's one reason divorce is so prevalent today. I now see in all my failures God's divine teaching is to prepare me for the finish. There is a purpose for my pain. I need to pay attention to that pain. Each day dawns because God gifts us the breath of life for one more day. The end of the race is nearer than any of us think. Our lives on earth are a mist, a mere vapor.

I want to be one of those old gray-haired saints who only cares about Jesus and people—just give me Jesus and help me love my neighbors. I want to grow old with Jesus, as the "love bucket" that my daughter says I am today. Accomplishments, like wealth and success, come and go. I want to be the woman God has called me to be. A woman whose identity and purpose are in Christ. What I didn't know, but was about to learn, was how to reflect God's love in my relationships.

CHAPTER TEN

RELATIONSHIPS IN CHRIST

Rooting my identity and purpose in Jesus taught me the most important relationship in my life is my relationship with God. The first and greatest commandment in the Bible is to love God. The second is to love others. We have seen that our identity is in Christ, and he wants us to reflect to the world who he is. We know from the Bible that God is love, and he created us to love us. But the love that God creates us for is not primarily for him to get satisfaction from us. Instead, God gives us the privilege of being satisfied in him because nothing else will bring us greater joy.

> "Teacher, which is the great commandment in the Law?" And [Jesus] said to him, "You shall love the Lord your God with all your heart and with all your soul and with all your mind. This is the great and first commandment. And a second is like it: You shall love your neighbor as yourself. On these two commandments depend all the Law and the Prophets." (Matthew 22:36–40)

So, we are to love God wholeheartedly, and the commandment to love our neighbor is "like it." Loving each other is like loving God. It is the mark of a true Christian and, when we love one another, we are showing the world that we are Jesus's followers.

> A new commandment I give to you, that you love one another: just as I have loved you, you also are to love one another. By this all people will know that you are my disciples, if you have love for one another. (John 13:34–35)

We are all called to be in relationship with God and others through love. Love lives in relationships. God didn't create man to be alone and lonely (Genesis 2:18). We all desire wholeness, and the heart of wholeness is connection—connection to God and others. Connect to God and reflect him by loving him and loving others because this is the greatest commandment and the ultimate measure of our true happiness.

- "This is my commandment, that you love one another as I have loved you" (John 15:12).
- "So we have come to know and to believe the love that God has for us. God is love, and whoever abides in love abides in God, and God abides in him" (1 John 4:16).
- "I . . . urge you to walk in a manner worthy of the calling to which you have been called, with all humility and gentleness, with patience, bearing with one another in love" (Ephesians 4:1–2).
- "Above all, keep loving one another earnestly, since love covers a multitude of sins" (1 Peter 4:8).

So, here I am, called to a right relationship with God and others through my connections in love, but how do I have and hold loving relationships? Loving other people unselfishly is a noble virtue, but how do I, as a sinfully imperfect person, love another person? How is a loving relationship even possible with people I don't like?

Jesus teaches us to love our enemies and pray for those who persecute us (Matthew 5:44). I don't think this means that I must have deep personal relationships with every person I meet, but I need to love everyone, including my enemies. Following this teaching gives me liberating joy. Science and psychology prove that the best solution to conflict is reconciliation, and it's also what Jesus commands, as we see in the gospel of Matthew.

"If your brother sins against you, go and tell him his fault, between you and him alone. If he listens to you, you have gained your brother. But if he does not listen, take one or two others along with you, that every charge may be established by the evidence of two or three witnesses. If he refuses to listen to them, tell it to the church. And if he refuses to listen even to the church, let him be to you as a Gentile and a tax collector. Truly, I say to you, whatever you bind on earth shall be bound in heaven, and whatever you loose on earth shall be loosed in heaven. Again I say to you, if two of you agree on earth about anything they ask, it will be done for them by my Father in heaven. For where two or three are gathered in my name, there am I among them." (Matthew 18:15–20)

Reconciliation happens by communicating the truth in love, but you can only do that with God's supernatural grace and love. I didn't come to faith until shortly after the birth of my daughter in 2011. I met Mike's family in 2007. During the first few years of my relationships with Mike's family, I had a secular worldview. I didn't understand how or why people could be so unkind and unloving and express such cruel and unwarranted attacks. I didn't have the "universal sin" perspective when Mike's family mistreated me, and because I didn't have God's truth or love in me, I responded to threats of danger by running and hiding. My reaction to conflict was self-destructive. I was living with a worldly perspective and responding to adversity in my strength, according to my will, trying to control something I had no control over—the other person's sin condition.

During our blended family issues, I often told Mike that his family was not any different from my family. He always took offense to that because he thought my family was nothing like his—nonabusive, unaddicted, educated, law-abiding. But, over the years, Mike's opinion about his family has changed. During one of his family reunions, a family member betrayed and hurt him in the same way I experienced. The wound cut deep, and it was then when he realized his family was not any different from my family.

In part, I know Mike sees things differently now because he, too, has a personal and loving relationship with God. A relationship he didn't have in five-plus decades as a devout Catholic. In all those years of Catholic education, Mike was never (not even once) encouraged to read the Bible. Mostly he recited memorized prayers without having a personal relationship with God.

After our baptism at Saddleback and our spiritual family's encouragement to read the Bible, Mike and I now have a personal relationship with God and an understanding of his truth. God's truth allows us to see so clearly that we are all sinners. When you see life from that perspective, it changes everything. Your hurt doesn't change, but how you respond to it does.

Home should be a safe and nurturing place with unity, love, and honesty flowing from comfort, support, and encouragement. Most people want acceptance and unconditional love. Yet, few of us will accept others' flaws and imperfections, and we cannot, therefore, love them the way we should. An inability to accept other people for who they are creates less than ideal relationships. Because a family with sinfully imperfect people will never be perfect, to one degree or another, families today are disapproving, dysfunctional, divided, or divorced and, sometimes, dangerous, even.

As a counselor, I see many people with troubled souls, but it's always the same root issue. Like the apostle Paul, people struggle to understand their actions and why they continue to do things they know are wrong (Romans 7:15). God's truth is critical to confronting and understanding the consequences of sinful, even disastrous choices that people make. If I continued to respond to conflict by looking for a hole to crawl into, I would never be free. This self-imposed exile and shutdown is a tragic reality for many victims of abuse and bullying.

Jesus inspires me to work out my conflicts through truth-in-love communication. When I swallow my pride and dig deep to acknowledge, accept, and own my sin, I can face my fears head on and experience liberating joy. Jesus shows me how to put on my big girl pants, take the log out of my eye, and stop pointing the finger of blame at others. Conflict, at its core, is about unmet needs. My needs are unmet, and another person's needs are unmet. So what are my needs and part in this?

In our ministry at the Family Peace Center, we teach that the best way to have and hold healthy, loving relationships is to share and care. We teach our kids and counseling clients that they must reveal to heal if they want to resolve conflicts. It is life-changing to take the truth of the gospel and teach people what sin is. We're not supposed to abuse, lie, hurt, or disrespect each other, but to varying degrees, we all do this to one another because of our sin condition.

Christians stand for truth and love. We seek the truth, and we strive to love. To the extent possible, Christians should respect, encourage, accept, and love one another. Jesus taught me how to Be R.E.A.L. with people, and this has shaped how Mike and I raise our daughter, how we minister to others at the Family Peace Center, and how we communicate with and relate to our spiritual family and neighbors.

- Respect—Honor all people, because a human soul is more valuable than worldly wealth.
- Encourage—Share words and deeds of affirmation with every person in your life.
- Accept—Allow for imperfection with compassion and forgiveness and do not judge others.
- Love—Offer kindness and mercy in every relationship.

Jesus teaches me to take time to get to know those I love. He encourages me to share my life and care about their lives. So, I try to be present and show interest in people. I want to treat others with respect and try to encourage, accept, and love them because healthy, God-honoring relationships are for all people, even those who don't love (or like) me in return.

I'm not perfect at this, but I'm improving, because I believe things such as taking the time to look a friend in the eye and asking them about their lives in a happy and affirming way are important. God created us for connection, and our relationship with him is the most important we will ever have. If I find it hard to talk to someone, I ask God to help me.

I don't expect to perfect at this in my earthly life, but to the extent possible, I no longer fight or run and hide from conflict. That's because walking with Jesus changes everything. So, I face adversity head on, communicating the truth with my adversaries in love.

There will always be peculiarities about people that annoy me because, as fallen humans, we are all flawed. Further, when we live together with imperfect people, our aggravation and impatience with others rise because we are living with people who irritate us and differ from us. If you have children, you know well how they are experts at pushing your buttons. Whether living together as a family inside your home or other people living outside your home, selfish sinners have unique personalities and interests. Put people together for any period, and tensions will brew.

If you have a secular worldview, you will never understand or accept this. You will fight the rest of your life trying to prove that you are right in your conflict because, without Jesus, your pride says that it's more important to be right than to do what's right. Selfish people focus on who is right. Unselfish people focus on what is right. God wants us to love one another. Relational harmony is possible because our sin problem becomes God's mercy through his love for us.

God also calls us to encourage people to build them up (1 Thessalonians 5:11). So, I do this, trying hard not to exclude anyone. I'm able to do this with the overflow of God's love for me. It's easy for me to love and encourage others, and I do it every day in a hundred unique ways. I see the good in life and people, and I praise and compliment the people I know often.

One way I do this is through a greeting card ministry I started just after coming to faith. I custom-print cards with a personalized, typed sentiment, and meaningful message to inspire, encourage, and bless people I know. Over the last ten years, I have delivered over five hundred cards to family, friends, and acquaintances.

I try to share the overflow of God's love to all the people he places in my life, but it only makes sense that some will not be interested in me or my attempts to encourage or love them. In the same way, it's only natural that I will not like everyone I meet. But that's okay because I don't think God intends that I go the distance with every person I know throughout my life. And let's be honest. How many real, 24-7, lay-their-life-down-for-you friends do you have? I only need one hand to count mine.

I couldn't do this before I met Jesus, but now, if someone rejects my love or encouragement, I pray for them and love them, even if— and this is key—even if they don't like me in return. My prayer for people who reject me is to ask God to help me love them the way he loves them and see them through the eyes of Jesus. For unbelievers, I pray that God will work in their lives to open their hearts so they can experience authentic love. I don't fight, run, hide, wish them ill will, or harbor bitter resentment.

I do this because Jesus calls me to do so, and his light overcame my darkness. Showing love to someone without having a deep relationship with them is a general call to love. The parable of the good Samaritan (Luke 10:25–37) helped me see to "love our neighbors" means that we can show love to people we don't know through a close relationship.

I realize not everyone I meet wants a deep personal relationship with me. And I don't want that closeness with everyone I meet either. There are many professional or functional relations in our lives, such as doctors, teachers, students, household contractors, etc. We don't necessarily have close relationships with these people, though we can if we choose.

Meaningful relationships take time and effort to nurture and grow. Relationships are not an event. It's not like you make a great connection and are good to go until happily ever after. Warm, trusting, and loving relationships require an investment of time and a genuine concern and interest in the other person. If you desire a more meaningful connection with someone, your goal has to reach above civility and superficiality beyond just knowing a few personal things about them and asking obligatory questions, such as "How are things going?" Casual "hi" and "bye" and "how's the weather" niceties produce nothing more than elevator-ride acquaintances.

There are now over 7.8 billion people living on Planet Earth. My goal is not to have a personal relationship with everyone (that's impossible). Still, Jesus teaches that we can have concentric circles of increasingly intimate personal relationships. Jesus sent seventy-two into every place where he was about to go (Luke 10:1). Then, there were the twelve disciples Jesus appointed to be with him (Mark 3:14). Inside that circle of twelve were Peter, James, and John, the disciples Jesus was closer to and took with him onto the Mount of Transfiguration (Matthew 17:1), into the house where he raised the child (Luke 8:51), and then into the garden of Gethsemane (Mark 14:33). Finally, there is John, who is widely known as "the disciple whom Jesus loved" (John 19:26; 20:2; 21:7; 21:20).

So, Jesus himself had an outer court and an inner court of personal relationships in varying depths—yet these "insiders" didn't become exclusive to the love he had for all "outside." Jesus had close personal relationships with the inner circle, but he was genuine and kindhearted toward all. That's my goal. Following Jesus helps me get there. We will have inner and outer friend circles, but like the Good Samaritan, Jesus calls us to love all people, even those not deeply connected to us.

Relationships get complicated when it requires loving our enemies. It's one thing to ask me to love someone who doesn't want to know me personally. That seems somewhat of a minor offense compared to someone who, either unintentionally or deliberately, hurts me. Does Jesus expect me to love people who hurt me, namely my enemies? The answer is yes; he does. Our goal is love.

Love is the fruit of the Spirit. The Holy Spirit only comes to us through faith, and our faith endures through God's truth. God's truth shows his love's depths—all God's promises through the crucifixion of his Son for our sins come from this love. From the mind of the apostle Paul, when we have love for one another, we are fulfilling all of God's teachings (Romans 13:8). Love is our endgame in all relationships.

Before I met Jesus, I wore a mask. I was trying to be perfect on the outside, but I was empty on the inside. Emptiness holds so much. Imprisonment inside walls of my loneliness separated me from authentic relationships and the love I needed. Loving people authentically wasn't apparent to me immediately after coming to faith, but slowly, one revelation at a time, Jesus taught me something that changed my life. Jesus showed me what real love means. He showed me the aim in relationships, and life is love, and though I understood and followed this teaching, I didn't know there was something more profound required to experience love in the fullest sense, but I was about to learn.

CHAPTER ELEVEN

FORGIVENESS IN CHRIST

And now we come to one hallmark of the Christian faith—forgiveness. Often regarded as one of the most hard-to-embrace Christian morals, this saintly virtue incites universal opposition from Christ-followers and nonreligious alike. Forgiveness is a weighty topic easily misunderstood in its complexity. So how do we make sense of this paradox about forgiveness? Is it a curse of our fallen world that we accept as unchangeable, or is it something to pursue because, ultimately, it will bless us?

There is nothing frivolous about forgiveness. Forgiveness will cost you. It cost Jesus his life. Following the man who bore the soul-crushing weight of the sins of the world cannot happen apart from trouble and sorrow. I cannot claim to be a true Christian and be free from suffering. Contrary to our contemporary culture, Jesus doesn't coddle; he confronts, convicts, and converts. I needed to swallow hard to hear his words *love your enemies*, and then I prayed like this:

> Our Father in heaven,
> hallowed be your name.

> Your kingdom come,
> your will be done,
>   on earth as it is in heaven.
> Give us this day our daily bread,
> and forgive us our debts,
>   as we also have forgiven our debtors.
> And lead us not into temptation,
>   but deliver us from evil.
> For if you forgive others their trespasses,
> your heavenly Father will also forgive you.
>   (Matthew 6:9–14)

In my natural self, apart from Jesus, I wanted to be strong. If someone wronged me, I instinctively wanted to retaliate—an eye-for-an-eye and a tooth-for-a-tooth. To me, admitting I was wrong was a sign of weakness. But then Jesus showed me a countercultural way to respond to my adversaries. Jesus teaches us not to repay evil for evil but to repay evil with good (Romans 12:17) and bless our enemies (1 Peter 3:9). Jesus calls us to forgiveness through humility in loving our enemies (Luke 6:27–35).

Humility should comfort our soul more than the gratification of pride. Jesus wants us to become as humble as children and willing to be the least of all (Matthew 18:4) and (Matthew 20:26). The best way to forgive someone is to humble yourself.

Shortly after relocating to the East Coast, I volunteered to serve as a children's teacher at a community Bible study group. Sharing personal stories of how individuals came to faith was common in the church and Bible study I was attending. Agreeing to share my story after receiving an invitation from my church and Bible study group, I put pen to paper and began writing.

I didn't think I could accurately depict what coming to know Jesus was like after living five decades in a life without faith, but nothing is impossible with God. After reflecting on where I had been before Jesus, I felt freedom and understood firsthand 2 Corinthians 3:16: "When one turns to the Lord, the veil is removed." It wasn't long after boldly sharing my story that the layers of the onion began peeling.

A few months after my Bible study session ended, I received a letter from my dad, whom, at that point, I had not seen in over ten years. My parents were still alive, but in failing health. They wanted to see me. I froze when I received the letter, but remembered God was with me now and I didn't need to fear my dad any longer. Once again, I put pen to paper and shared my heart, telling them I did not want to see them but wished them no ill will. I told them I was a Christian following Jesus and offered them a plan of salvation so they, too, could be free from their brokenness and bondage to sin. I prayed for my parents, mailed my letter, and thought that was the end of that.

By now, I was reading the Bible and listening to audiobooks and sermons daily, attending church and Bible studies regularly, and serving in multiple ministries. I was also hosting community groups in my home while following several online preaching and teaching Christian leaders, all while pursuing distance learning certification for pastoral care ministry ordination. Renewing my mind by saturating my life in God's Word was an intentional spiritual discipline that I practiced daily in my obedience to follow Jesus.

It wasn't long after sending my letter to my parents that echoes of Matthew 5:24, "leave your gift there before the altar and go. . . . Be reconciled," began stirring in my soul, and soon I reached out to my stepdaughters and in-laws to make peace. One by one, I met face-to-face with family members to say, "I'm sorry," and to ask, "Will you forgive me?"

Twelve family members, thirteen if you count Mike's mom—yes, it's possible, and healthy, to forgive people who have passed away. Mike's family all live out-of-state, so it was a long process. Mike sat beside me with each encounter, scratching his head, wondering why I (who he believed was the victim and not the perpetrator in these offenses) was apologizing.

As we were preparing for one of our destinations, I asked Mike if we could make a stop and add my parents to the list of those I needed to forgive. I remember Mike looking confused, but no one was more surprised by this than me. Lacking an ability to articulate why I was doing this, it felt as if I were going through robotic motions, but I knew enough about Jesus to trust him.

So with little more than my faith and trust in Jesus, Mike, my daughter, and I headed to Chicago to visit my parents. It was a two-day visit. The first night we met at a restaurant. After introducing my parents to my husband and daughter, I looked them in their eyes, hugged them, asked for their forgiveness, and let them know I forgave them. It was the hardest thing I've ever done. It was also the most God-honoring and life-giving.

The next day we went to their apartment for a cordial visit. After our time together, we hugged and said goodbye. That was the last time I ever saw my mom. Nine months after that visit, my mom passed away. During the months following our visit and before my mom died, we spoke on the phone periodically, trying our best to navigate our new relationship. I was conflicted on so many levels, but I knew God was holding and healing my heart.

I remember feeling a knot in my stomach and profound sorrow after receiving the news that my mom had passed. Half relief, half shame welled inside me. I felt relief from knowing I was now free from the haunting guilt that I could never give my mom what she needed. I felt shame because my mom needed me in the same way I needed my daughter—she looked to me to fill her emptiness just as I looked to my daughter to heal my wounds. Like my dad, my mom didn't love me for who I was as much as she loved me for what she needed.

God reminded me that my identity is in him, and when I root my identity in Christ, I see that God created me for connection through relationships with him and others. I was sorrowful because I didn't have a genuine connection with my mom, but God showed me how to rejoice in sorrow. I'm grateful that God is teaching me not to look to my daughter for what I need but seeing her for the person God made.

To honor my mom's life, I wrote a prayer thanking God for my mom and her love for me. I shared my gratitude that God opened my heart to forgive my mom so I could see her before she passed away because it brought her peace to see me safe and happily married to a good man with a child to nurture. I confessed that I didn't know if my mom believed in God, and I was unclear about what happens to nonbelievers when they pass away, but I prayed for her salvation so I can see her again in heaven.

Rolling the printed prayer into a glass bottle, I went to a beach near my home with a friend where we set it afloat in the Atlantic Ocean. And so, rather than living with the regret that I never made peace with my mom, God gave me this gift. I remember feeling closer to Jesus during this season of loss, more than any other time up to that point in my faith journey.

One reason I could ask my parents and Mike's family for their forgiveness was because I realized they didn't hurt me. I hurt myself. The most significant revelation was learning how I hurt myself. I hurt myself because I allowed other people to mean more to me than God. I didn't know this until I met Jesus, but it doesn't matter what other people think of me or do to me.

If you live for people's approval, you will die by their criticism, as the saying goes. What matters is who God says I am, and how God feels about me, how God loves me, and how God's victory on Calvary conquers my battles. Jesus already carried that cross—the one that forgave all my sins. Forgiveness isn't about me; it's about God.

During one of my reconciliations with Mike's family, I recall asking for forgiveness, saying I was sorry and confessing that I was selfish and only thinking about myself. I remember feeling surprised by the reaction I received to what I thought was a sincerely heart-wrenching apology. My words seemed to provoke an intense response from the other person, fueled mostly by anger.

I remember a spirited discourse reaching a fervent pitch, and when cooler heads prevailed, I tried to explain that I forgive others because I have Jesus in my life now. I recall that the other person didn't see things that way but instead thought I forgave because motherhood made me a softer and more forgiving person. That is possible, and I can see why someone might see it that way, but that isn't why.

The reason I forgive is that, in the end, I get Jesus. He is more beautiful and brings more joy to me than anyone or anything else in this world. I love Jesus with all my heart and unequal affection. Above all else, Jesus is the one who won my heart. He teaches me how to be free from sin within my enchanted prison, where I war daily against wicked worldly messages inside my heartland battleground.

My intent in sharing these stories is not to defile anyone's character, and this is the evidence that I've been born again, that God is in my life now. Until I met Jesus, I wasn't able to show mercy to other people, let alone give them the grace or the love that God has given me. Life is sacred, and all people deserve dignity. Every tribe, nation, people group, creed, color, and race deserve dignity. I believe people at their core want good and want God in their life, but they cannot do good and surrender their pride and desire for control, without the saving grace and love of Jesus.

Being able to forgive so many people, including myself, is the reality of God's power in my life because before I met Jesus, forgiveness was not something I could do. Who possesses power like that? Matthew 5:11–12 says, "Blessed are you when others revile you and persecute you and utter all kinds of evil against you falsely on my account. Rejoice and be glad, for your reward is great in heaven." I learned that not only can I withstand people's mistreatment when they hurl all kinds of evil and false accusations at me, but I can also rejoice and be glad in it because I get the prize. I get Jesus.

Forgiving so many people was a long and painful obedience, but it started with owning my sin. Only after I admitted and was accountable for my sin, could I forgive—sixteen people in total—three people from my family of origin (my parents and my deceased uncle) and thirteen people from my family-by-marriage.

Forgiveness was hard for me because it's unnatural. Sin-stricken people love the darkness. John 3:19, says, "This is the judgment: the light has come into the world, and people loved the darkness rather than the light because their works were evil."

Admitting how foolish and selfish I was to my enemies was a big pill to swallow. Every fiber of my being wanted to war rather than surrender my pride, and I didn't care if that meant my relationship would suffer the collateral damage. But even more than all that, the biggest reason forgiveness was so hard for me was that I felt if I admitted wrongdoing and apologized, it would seem as if I wasn't ever hurt. And I wanted people to know they hurt me. I wanted revenge. But Jesus taught me that vengeance doesn't belong to me; vengeance belongs to God.

Jesus's words to overcome evil with good (Romans 12:21) shocked and offended me when I first heard them, but I've since learned that

I play a much smaller role in this than I thought. I need only return good for evil and bless those who have wronged me. That's it. That's my responsibility toward my enemies, and I can do it whether my offender admits wrong or not.

I leave the weight of punishment to God because he will judge justly. When we repay evil with good, God sees how perfectly we reflect Jesus. When we connect to God and reflect him, he sees our efforts to offer forgiveness as generous and gracious. Also, God promises that if we forgive others, he will forgive us (Matthew 6:14).

The parable of the unmerciful servant (Matthew 18:21–35) shows me how freely I was living by God's mercy and forgiveness, yet I was so unwilling to forgive others. I needed to give all of that to God and trust that he would take care of the justice. When I thought more about this, I realized that seeking revenge would only intensify the offense. Also, anything I could do would pale compared to God's justice.

God will justly condemn better than I ever could because he punishes all sin. Nobody goes unpunished. God's justice is the promise that freed me from an unforgiving, bitter, and vengeful spirit. Every wrongdoing, no matter how small, is part of God's plan for our lives. God allows trials and offenses in our lives so that our faith might be tested and proven. Jesus was nailed to a cross to die for us. His suffering was for sin—not his own, but ours. He left an example so we might follow in his steps. Through God's preparation, we discover our true identity, and that truth sets us free.

Our love toward others should be free of accusation, faultfinding, and blame shifting. Jesus teaches accusers who point the finger of blame toward others a great lesson about forgiveness in the story of the woman caught in adultery: "Jesus stood up and said to her, 'Woman, where are they? Has no one condemned you?' She said, 'No one, Lord.' And Jesus said, 'Neither do I condemn you; go, and from now on sin no more'" (John 8:10–11).

Jesus knew his calling was to bring sinners to regret their sins, not to destroy them but to save them. The adulteress woman felt sorrow over her sin because Jesus showed her his mercy. The woman's accusers also felt shame because Jesus showed them their sins. They wanted to trap Jesus, but Jesus confronted, convicted, and converted them. This parable also teaches us we shouldn't interfere in work that doesn't belong to us. Vengeance is none of our business. Vengeance belongs to God. "I will repay, says the Lord" (Romans 12:19).

How can we undeservingly take God's forgiveness of our sins but not forgive someone who offends us? What does that say about our hearts? We can't authentically forgive anyone if we don't forgive from the heart. If we hold on to an unforgiving spirit, we won't be forgiven by God, because an unforgiving heart is an unforgiven heart.

Forgiving so many people was hard, but when I learned how to love my enemies, I realized I could have only done that through Jesus. I had to let Jesus hold my hand to walk me through an impossible problem I couldn't resolve on my own. When I did that, I secured my place in God's forever family. John 15:5 says, "I am the vine; you are the branches. Whoever abides in me and I in him, he it is that bears much fruit, for apart from me you can do nothing."

Of the sixteen people I forgave, only one reciprocated in kind by asking for my forgiveness for their wrongdoing. Many said nothing while most of the others defended their parts in the conflict, boldly proclaiming their innocence while pointing their fingers of blame toward me for all the wrongdoing. Conflict stems from opposing mindsets and closed hearts. People in conflict are out to get, not give.

When someone is unwilling to hear, respect, and accept another person's perspective in reconciliation, hearts harden, and minds close. It's as if one person says to the other, "You don't have a say in this. It's my way or the highway. And my way is always the right way."

We all have a voice or a "side" to the story. If you reach the point where someone is unwilling to listen to your side, attempts to reconcile will be futile until someone dares to speak the truth in love.

I had to humble myself and rise above pettiness and blame shifting. I had to take the log out of my eye and stop judging the spec in the other's person's eye and say, "I'm sorry that my words and actions hurt you. I was wrong. I was only being selfish and thinking about myself. Do you forgive me?"

What I learned was that even if the other person is unwilling to accept or offer forgiveness in return, God sees my willingness—and that's what matters. Galatians 6:7 says, "Do not be deceived: God is not mocked, for whatever one sows, that will he also reap." God sees everything, and he knows what is inside every heart. Jesus teaches that the integrity of our actions shown by our goodwill to forgive our enemies matters more than the outcome of what our obedience produced (2 Corinthians 8:10–12).

If others will not be receptive to my forgiveness, and if I don't always get the peace I'm looking for from my effort, then why forgive at all? We forgive because we get Jesus.

Forgiveness is not about us; forgiveness is about Jesus. Many things will follow an obedient call to forgiveness, like freedom from God's wrath, freedom from going to hell, and freedom from guilt, shame, bitterness, and anger—even knowing God's forgiveness of you because you forgave another. But the real prize is getting Jesus. He is our goal (1 Peter 3:18).

We forgive to honor God, not to honor others. Jesus warns us not to practice our righteousness so that others can see us as God-centered and affirm us. Jesus calls these people hypocrites whose hearts are not faithful to God. "And your Father who sees in secret will reward you" (Matthew 6:4).

The Bible tells us we should make peace with everyone in our lives, to the extent possible (Romans 12:18). As a Christian, I have done my part in what Jesus calls me to do through loving my enemies. Christians are to bless and love people who "revile . . . and utter all kinds of evil against" them (Matthew 5:11). If we love only those who love us, what reward do we have, and how will people look at the Christian faith as any different from faithless lives? (Matthew 5:46–47)

Among the many people God helped me forgive, I restored one relationship to a closer, more loving bond than we had before. I'm beyond grateful for this beautiful gift. But I never stopped loving those who did not warmly receive my offer of forgiveness. I blessed and prayed for them and then moved on.

God desires for us to establish healthy boundaries. If others don't want us in their lives, there is nothing we can do about that. We cannot change a heart; only God can. My job is to plant the seed. God supplies the increase. For me, moving on doesn't mean that I dispose, delete, or eradicate others from my life, and it doesn't mean

I stop loving or praying for them. It means that there is no bond with certain people, and there might always be a distance between us.

Trust is not the same as forgiveness. You can forgive someone, but it may take years to trust them, if ever again. You can't bear God's fruit before it's time, but God still calls us to forgive. I don't stop loving someone because they offended, disrespected, angered, disappointed, frustrated, or hurt me. I give all of that to God.

Some of these severed relationships hurt me deeply, and I wish I could tell you I discovered how to make that hurt go away. But as far as I have seen, there is nothing, on this side of eternity, that will ever take away that kind of hurt. If I could unhurt myself, I would, but I can't. Some wounds cut deeper than others and may always carry a scar. I can't change my hurt, but I can change the way I respond to it.

What's more, Jesus experienced every kind of suffering I have. Just as I experienced physical suffering at the hands of abusers, Jesus suffered physical pain, nailed and beaten on the cross. And Jesus suffered emotional pain when falsely accused of crimes he didn't commit, and his closest friends betrayed, abandoned, and denied him in his hour of need. I also suffered (and will continue to suffer) from people's rejection and unkind, unloving behaviors toward me. Jesus even knew deep spiritual suffering when his Father forsook him in his righteous anger against human sin, pouring his wrath out on him. I, too, felt abandoned by God when I couldn't see his presence in my life. So there's no experience of pain or suffering that Jesus cannot understand or heal.

Who could take a lost and broken-in-a-million-pieces person such as myself and transform my heart, so I now believe in a God who protects, nurtures, and provides for me in every way conceivable? God helped me to forgive those who hurt me. He changed the trajectory of my pitiful life so radically that I now help others in the same pain. Now I can love and be loved in healthy relationships and raise a child who knows God. Who else but a sovereign almighty God can do this?

Rebuilding broken families is God's business, and it's complicated, but it's never without hope. I used to be hopeless, but now I have faith. My new, forever family is not the family I was born into, and it isn't the family I married into, but it's the family I dreamed of as a girl. A family of people who gather with me in a place I call home. No longer a battleground, I now have a home surrounded with R.E.A.L. people who respect, encourage, accept, and love me.

Home is where all forgive. My home is with Jesus, and Jesus forgives me. It is here, with Jesus and my spiritual family, where I now live, not perfectly but powerfully, some days in sorrow, because in this life you will have trouble, but always rejoicing. I can rejoice in sorrow because even the worst of times on earth is only temporary. One day, I will wear a crown of perfection and walk with Jesus for eternity.

Are you surrendering your life to God? Or are you seeking to control it? Forgiveness, rightly understood, will change your life. I invite you to receive this life-giving gift. Once I learned about my identity, purpose, relationships, and forgiveness, there was just one more lesson Jesus wanted me to understand.

CHAPTER TWELVE

LEGACY IN CHRIST

There is a day coming when our lives on earth will be complete. Jesus teaches us to hold our worldly pleasures loosely because our lives are a fleeting season and our possessions are not ours anyway. When I live in faithful obedience to God my Father, and I treasure him above all else, I'm imitating Jesus and showing others the rich inheritance of eternity. "For what does it profit a man to gain the whole world and forfeit his soul?" (Mark 8:36)

A wise person once told me the greatest gift I can give my daughter is faith. For years I thought leaving a legacy meant documenting memories to create a keepsake for loved ones, something they could see and touch, so they would never forget where they came from and who they are. I've spent countless hours documenting my daughter's life milestones to memorialize our values so I can leave her a legacy. Every birthday, holiday, school year-end, ministry, or other significant event is artistically documented, reproduced, and gifted to family, friends, parents, teachers, and students who are part of our journey. My daughter has a rich and growing legacy of books, photos, and videos. While I think all of this is sweet and special and important, I have come to appreciate my friend's wisdom.

People don't leave legacies; they live legacies. Living a life of faith leaves an eternal legacy. The way I live out my faith in this life is how people will remember me when I depart to the next. It's how I'm living my faith—not sentimental keepsakes—that becomes the legacy I leave loved ones. Legacy is more than handing down a monetary inheritance or passing on values and a family name. I've never heard a dying man ask to see a copy of his bank statement—it's always about loved ones. People who are dying want to be surrounded by loved ones to impart words of wisdom for them to carry forward. Since Jesus is the founder and perfecter of our faith, what matters most is whether we connect and reflect Jesus in our lives. What we leave our loved ones is our faith in Jesus.

This wise person who schooled me on lessons of faith was married to an equally wise man. Mike and I met them in our Saddleback Church small group Bible study in 2011. The impact they had on my life was extraordinary. Pearl, taught me the significance of leaving my faith as my legacy, and Roger taught me how to live my faith. As a freshly baptized baby Christian, it was a blessing to have such mature believers in my new spiritual family. Roger and Pearl both grew up in Christian homes. As faith was modeled early in their lives, neither needed a "hitting rock bottom" experience before finding a firm foundation. The God-honoring lives they lived were as rock-solid a witness to Christ as I have ever seen.

Roger and Pearl showed me that I didn't need all my "How can I be sure God exists?" questions answered. Did I want to be sure? Of course. Did I want proof? Initially, yes. But through them, I realized that it wasn't scientific or philosophical proof I needed. The way they lived their lives was the evidence that silenced all my doubts. They showed me that there is a God amidst our daily lives. And this God wasn't surrounded by trumpet-blowing, white-winged creatures plucking harp strings. Instead, through their lives, I saw a God relentlessly pursuing us through our mess and misery in our secular world gone wrong, trying to show us his truth despite our blindness.

Our blindness comes from our preference for darkness over light (John 3:19). Left to ourselves, we will not see God's truth and beauty, so he intervenes, shining light in our hearts (2 Corinthians 4:6) to give us the strength to fight for holiness and faith.

One way God breaks through our blindness is by giving us spiritual sight in our new birth. God didn't create a sinless Christian in my new birth. When the light of Jesus came into my heart, God gave me different desires for holiness by showing me my pride and need for control. I became a sin-hating fighter, but I was still responsible for my moral preferences and proclivity to sin. Sometimes God shows us our rebellion and allows us to fail to redirect our sinful inclinations, but he never leaves us in our disobedience. No one born of God makes a practice of sinning (1 John 3:9).

Roger inspired Mike to read the Bible. Mike regards Roger as the spiritual mentor who changed his life. Roger was also one of my spiritual mentors, and I considered him my God-appointed earthly father. I adored Roger. His life touched me deeply. His humility, integrity, kindness, and compassion were without equal and endeared me to his eternal soul.

Roger passed away in 2015, but his legacy lives in me. He lived a simple but honest life. A man so humble that the mere mention of his humility embarrassed him. He was a real man with real problems. The pain and suffering and agony and defeat of countless health challenges never left him complaining. The trials and tribulations in personal and professional relationships left him without a bitter or scorned heart. He was faithful to God, his wife, family, and friends. He exemplified the Greatest Commandment. He and Pearl enjoyed fifty-nine years of marriage before he passed.

Marriage is a model of a profound spiritual truth to show us how we are to relate to God. No other relationship better illustrates our union with Christ. Marriage is one of God's highest callings, and Roger and Pearl's commitment to God and one another taught me why marriage matters. The example they showed me in their relationship with God and their relationship with each other strengthened my faith and my marriage.

A biblical expression of faith is seen in Hebrews 11:1, "Now faith is the assurance of things hoped for, the conviction of things not seen." Faith, unlike a sentimental material remembrance, is not something you can touch or see with the naked eye. "Hoped for" and "not seen" are key. Faith is the assurance of things hoped for, namely, Jesus in eternity, where he wipes away every tear from our eyes, with no more death, mourning, crying, or pain. Jesus is our only hope for eternal life. And the conviction of things not seen is, in fact, seen upon reflection of our lives.

God's footprint is everywhere in our lives. Our obedience to our faith in Jesus on earth is a shadow of things to come in eternity. God knows the plans he has for us, and they are "not for evil" but are plans for "a future and a hope" (Jeremiah 29:11). People often struggle to understand God's will for their lives because they can't see (with their physical eyes) his beautiful plans. But faith is a trust that comes from a spiritual sight through the eyes of our hearts. Even when we suffer and grieve, God promises to make all things right through our obedience and faith. Faith is not something you can see in plain sight, but you can undoubtedly see faith working in other people or even upon reflection of what God has brought you through.

Some mysteries of God are hidden, but most are not. They're there—we just need spiritual light and sight to see them. I couldn't see God's hand in my former life, but that doesn't mean he wasn't there. God is always with me, and whether you know it or not, he is always with you too. We will never be in a place where God isn't with us. God brought together all my past suffering for good, because there is a higher purpose in pain.

My story is unfolding through God's (Kairos) time, not my (Chronos) time. Kairos time is a series of moments and events that we see in our faith in God, whose hands mold our lives. Chronos time refers to a specific amount of time divided into minutes, hours, days, and weeks. My past life of pain brought me a heightened sensitivity and compassion to help others, which I now do through serving in a purposeful ministry. The world of hurt I endured through experiencing a myriad of blended family issues led me to Jesus and produced a beautiful child for me to love and nurture, giving me a more profound commitment to my marriage.

My girlhood dream to marry a farmer and have lots of children was realized through all of this. Mike is a man with the utmost integrity. He received the blessing that hard work begets success from his ancestors. He raised money to start and grow three successful businesses through his unwavering commitment to the ministry of excellence and dedication to building healthy relationships among his employees. His capacity to grow companies at breakneck speed, where other entrepreneurs would require a decade to accomplish similar outcomes, is astonishing. To observe the level of discipline and the commitment that it takes to do what he does is a blessing. His power portfolio and sustained success in amassing three prosperous start-ups would inflate any other person's ego, yet he carries humility.

Of his many virtues, perhaps the one I admire most is his inexhaustible generosity. Whether at home, at work, or in the community, everybody benefits from Mike's giving nature. Mike personifies the principle of sowing and reaping in how he treats people (2 Corinthians 9:6). At one of his annual holiday parties, I looked around a room full of a hundred-plus people and marveled at how he built that company from scratch, how he took something from nothing and made it platinum. I thought about the many people who had reaped the benefit of gainful employment because of the seeds he sowed to start companies. These companies are still prospering, providing families with economic prosperity and job security. He's defining a new generation of corporate leaders by mentoring and grooming younger employees to live a legacy for these individuals to continue to grow the company for even more people to thrive. Everything Mike touches grows. He is God's gardener and my farmer.

One of my roles at the Family Peace Center is children's director, where I get the enormous privilege to teach and love on kids in my ministry. In 2018, our ministry opened, and we had eight students. The following year, we had ten. To say I love these children like my own is an understatement. These kids bring me immeasurable joy. I have as much love for them as my heart can hold. So, I married my farmer and had lots of children—the beginning of an end to my girlhood dream. Only a God of such amazing grace could have done that.

We all have a hunger that will never be satisfied until we let God's light shine in our hearts. Real seeing comes from God through spiritual light. L.I.G.H.T. Living in God's holy truth is the lamp to our feet. Many, not all, people today lack imagination. Where are the "big dreamers" like Martin Luther King Jr.? Now *there* was a courageous visionary who lived an eternal legacy! Billy Graham was another rock-solid, godly man of faith. Where are those bold, faith-filled heroes of today? Where are the godly men and women who live and leave indelible legacies of faith for us to imitate?

Newer generations are growing up with instant gratification and on-demand expectancy. You create it for me, and I will click it. If I don't like it, I can unfriend, thumbs down, or delete it until something more appealing catches my eye. Everything in our world today is disposable, including relationships. Have we lost our God-given gift of imagination to see the beauty of the unseen? Possibilities escape people living in lazy, entitled, self-serving arrogance and expectancy. Life can sometimes imitate art, as in a five-act dramatic play structure.

Act 1: The Exposition—the audience learns the setting, the characters develop, and a conflict begins. I can see this in my life. I was born at a particular time and place, surrounded by people who raised me where amidst all of that, my struggle ensued.

Act 2: Rising Action—complications and obstacles begin to emerge. The parallel in my life was my inexhaustible search for love and acceptance, which gave rise to unworthy feelings and tragic outcomes when withheld.

Act 3: The Climax—the play's turning point characterized by the highest amount of suspense. The turning point for me was my hopeless despair when I wanted to end my life, which all culminated in my saving faith in Jesus.

Act 4: Falling Action—gives clues that the story is ending with revealing plot twists. I see this where I'm living now, walking and falling, serving in humble obedience to live God's will, which continues to reveal twists that happen when I surrender to God's time, allowing his will be done, not my will. Even when I don't understand his will or when it involves suffering that I would rather not endure. In my life now, I'm striving to reach the mountaintop, climbing with my believing and unbelieving friends that God brings to journey along-side me.

Act 5: Resolution—reveals the outcome of the drama. And this will be the moment I am swept up to my forever home with Jesus in eternity. The final curtain will fall, revealing the cause of all my works on earth. My obedience to Jesus in this life is part of the next life because I lived my legacy here on this earth in faith, and that will pass to people whose lives I touched, whom I will see again in heaven.

I had a choice to make when I left my past life. Would I stay in the cycle of abuse, or would I become the transitional generation to save the next? I chose to be the transitional generation. I'm living that out in my faith now. My daughter sees the way I live, and my example will pass to her and anyone else God brings to me through my ministry, family, and friend circles.

I know people who are dying, and not all of them are believers. People who don't know Jesus handle death differently than my believing friends. Pearl, my dearest and closest friend, has a fatal disease that affects her brain and muscle control. She's losing her ability to walk, talk, and eat. It's a horrible way to die, but she's handling it with grace and dignity because she's looking forward to her homecoming with Jesus. This amazing woman of God is passing on untold seeds of faith for all those (and there are many) surrounding her in her last days.

As I write this, we are in the early days of lockdown. I'm not able to be by Pearl's side because of the air travel restrictions. I called her this week to say goodbye—we both knew my phone call was the last time we would speak. I told her I was writing the final chapter of my book. Before we hung up the phone, she told me she would see me in heaven. Then she told me to bring my book with me. She asked me to say goodbye to Mike and our daughter. I was grateful that we shared our deep mutual affection and love for one another, and then that was that.

In the end, this is all we have—our love for one another and our love for Jesus. Of all the people Jesus has brought to journey with me, Roger and Pearl have had the most significant impact on my spiritual life. They opened my eyes to Jesus in unforgettable ways. I loved their spiritual gifts and their life work. Their physical presence enriched my life and strengthened my faith in indescribable ways. I will miss Pearl (as I have Roger) dearly and deeply, but she's right—I will see her (and Roger) in heaven. And this is the hope Jesus brings.

After Jesus told the disciples what they had to do for eternal life, many no longer walked with him: "Jesus said to the twelve, 'Do you want to go away as well?' Simon Peter answered him, 'Lord, to whom shall we go? You have the words of eternal life, and we have believed, and have come to know, that you are the Holy One of God'" (John 6:67–69).

I ask myself the same question, To whom shall I go? Jesus is the only life I have. He's my only option, and he's your only option. We don't have another life. We don't have anyone or any place to return to but to Jesus and heaven.

And while we sit with God's truth in our lap, people are perishing. All around us. People who have never known Jesus, which means not only have they never experienced true joy, but they also will never get to heaven. When we get past the pandemic, it's only a matter of time before we will experience another crisis, causing us to face our mortality. And another after that.

There are millions of lost souls wandering toward self-destruction. What legacy do you want to live for your loved ones? Does your life reflect that you know Jesus? If not, I invite you to open your Bible and seek God's truth and give serious thought and prayer to your life goals and legacy.

Jesus inspires me to be a woman with gospel-rooted accountability to speak his truth and love the lost. It's easy for me to do this. I want to please God because I love God. It's not in my strength that I achieve my goals; it's God who is working in me.

> Therefore, my beloved, as you have always obeyed, so now, not only as in my presence but much more in my absence, work out your own salvation with fear and trembling, for it is God who works in you, both to will and to work for his good pleasure. (Philippians 2:12–13)

I labor toward this goal every day because I love Jesus. I want to share Jesus with others in the same way grandparents love their grandchildren and want to share them (and the many pictures they have of them) with others. Affection for something we love dearly causes us to want to share our joy with others so they can experience it too. I do this by sharing Jesus at home, within my family and friend circles, and through the Family Peace Center. All I did was open a door in my community to offer the life-giving gift of God's truth and love. And the flock unfolded.

Today, I counsel people in the mess of their lives and help them try to untangle their sins until they see Christ's beauty. I teach children how much Jesus loves them, and I write about Jesus's truth and love. I'm also a wife, mother, friend, and homemaker. Admittedly, my days are full.

Many people tell me they think I work too hard. They say I should slow down and not push myself too much. I recall telling someone that I just love Jesus and want to spread my passion for him to others, to which this person sympathetically asked, "Yes, but what do you do for you?" This person trying to express genuine concern for me said something to the effect that no one appreciates my efforts, and I was laboring in vain because people are taking advantage of me, and I'm getting nothing in return.

Jesus lives in me, and he is at work in me. What I do to live my life of obedience to Jesus is not a hardship. I'm not under threat. It's an honor and joy. The apostle Paul teaches, "By the grace of God I am what I am, and his grace toward me was not in vain. On the contrary, I worked harder than any of them, though it was not I, but the grace of God that is with me" (1 Corinthians 15:10).

God's Word makes us wise. I want to linger in the presence of God and hear his wisdom. There is no other person I could turn to that would give me such fruitful discernment and truth about life than God. God helped me endure a hard fight to survive decades of pain and confusion, and he brought me through all that to share his truth with others in the hope that they might meet the one who won my heart. Perhaps, if you open your heart, he will win yours too.

We have the story of Jesus to tell to lost souls within our reach. We need not travel to a third world country to find our mission field. Our mission field is within our homes and communities. Let's "run with endurance the race that is set before us" and "not grow weary or fainthearted" (Hebrews 12:1, 3). We need more storytellers to keep telling the story of Jesus.

Lord Jesus, bring us your lost sheep and help us tell your story because your story is our story. My confidence is that you recognize yourself through this writing because there is something for everyone when God speaks. My prayer is that God will use this book to bring you into his light in a new or deeper relationship with him so you will "not walk in darkness, but will have the light of life" to live a legacy of faith (John 8:12). Discovering my identity through God's preparation is not just my story. What's left is to see how my story and God's story becomes our story, and the ultimate meaning of life.

PART THREE

OUR STORY

CHAPTER THIRTEEN

OUR STORY

I spent five decades searching for truth, love, kindness, and compassion. I found it all when I met Jesus, finally quenching that lifelong thirst—the truth did, in fact, set me free (John 8:32).

In this book, I share personal insights in five areas of life fundamental to understanding God's truth:

1. What's your identity? You're a God-created person made in the image of Christ who connects with and reflects Jesus.
2. What's the purpose of your life? To connect with and reflect Jesus while serving others through obedience.
3. How do you have and hold loving relationships? Connecting with and reflecting Jesus in order to love God and love others.
4. How do you forgive the unforgivable? By connecting with and reflecting Jesus in humility to love your enemies.
5. How do you live a lasting legacy? By connecting with Jesus in love and reflecting your faith in him to show the world his infinite beauty.

It's all about Jesus. He is the answer to everything. If you desire truth, wisdom, joy, and a plan of salvation for your eternal life, you need Jesus. We have all gone astray. Jesus changes people. I love Jesus and the truth that he reveals to me in his written Word, the Bible. Jesus's teaching about sin is life-changing. I'm grateful for that knowledge. Jesus says, "My people are destroyed for lack of knowledge" (Hosea 4:6).

We can all grow in new understandings. I want to live and love well, but I also want to grieve and suffer well. The character of God shows us he is a God of emotions. He delights in his Son. He delights in justice and righteousness. He rejoices in his people. He takes pleasure in himself, his ways, his grace, and his people's obedience. He grieves and experiences pain and sorrow. He weeps and he experiences anger. God is compassionate and loving. Our identities are rooted in the image of God, so we have emotions too. We're not robots. Oh, God, help us live well, love well, grieve well, and suffer well because we want to live full, complete lives, with you by our sides.

When I began serving in the Saddleback Church children's ministry, I heard a student tell her story about how God saved her life. After hearing her testimony of faith, a journey to discover who God is in my life began that continues to this day. I wouldn't know this girl if she walked through my front door today. A stranger spoke a word from God, planting a seed in me through a God-ordained, Kairos moment that changed my life.

Seeds hold miraculous potential to reproduce infinitely, and that's what Jesus calls all of us to do in the Great Commission—Go and make disciples of all the nations. Spread the good news of the gospel. Plant the seed (connect with and reflect God), cultivate the soil (love God, love others, live your legacy in your faith in Jesus), and God will supply the increase of the harvest.

There are many unexpected situations in my life and relationships that don't go the way I would like. Sometimes I want a deeper connection with a person who wants nothing to do with me. And sometimes, that makes me upset or frustrated and even hurt sometimes. When that happens, I pray for God to show me what he sees, and if it isn't clear, I ask him for patience to see what his better purpose is.

Usually, when I wait and reflect, I can see a seed that just needs time to harvest—in God's time, Kairos time, not my chronological time. I don't know why it took me sixty years to write my life story, but God knew. And this isn't just my story, it's God's story, and God's story is our story.

We're all gifted uniquely. Jesus teaches me not to compare my gifts to other people. He empowers me to be the most God-centered, mission-advancing, others-serving person I can be, and he gives me the strength to be that person, to seek and serve the lost with his love, and to live my legacy.

I want to be and accomplish all that God created me for:

- to love God, above all else;
- to honor my marriage and love my husband without judgment;
- to unconditionally love and raise our daughter;
- to be R.E.A.L. (respectful, encouraging, accepting, and loving) toward all people God brings into my life; and
- to serve others with love—forgiving them with grace and speaking to them in truth.

Jesus roots me in love, and my faith anchors me in his truth. More than a dry, academic theology, this is a life-altering theology, and this is my life—to live in light. No longer living in "fear of man" (Proverbs 29:25), I confess my sins in this book, inviting you to see who I am in all my flawed humanity and open the door to share how living in God's holy truth (L.I.G.H.T.) changes everything.

Revealing painful and unflattering truths about myself is not easy. Through God's grace, I pray it is helpful. Only God can transform lives, but the means he often uses are the stories of his work in other believers' lives. My prayer is that God will use something in this book to awaken your heart to a deeper faith. Or if you're not walking in faith, my prayer is that you ask God into your life, so you, too, can connect with and reflect Jesus and drink from the "rivers of living water" (John 7:38).

If a voice is whispering in your heart, take comfort that this is Jesus calling you out of darkness into his light. Connecting with and reflecting God is our aim, and anything that brings you to him will bear fruit. Answer his call and take his hand. He will never let you go.

Born of darkness
And this is the judgment: the light has come into the world, and people loved the darkness rather than the light because their works were evil. (John 3:19)

To wander wounded
For you were straying like sheep, but have now returned to the Shepherd and Overseer of your souls. (1 Peter 2:25)

We die in light
But if we walk in the light, as he is in the light, we have fellowship with one another, and the blood of Jesus his Son cleanses us from all sin. (1 John 1:7)

To rise in freedom
If we confess our sins, he is faithful and just to forgive us our sins and to cleanse us from all unrighteousness.
(1 John 1:9)

Born of darkness, to wander wounded, we die in light to rise in freedom. Will you continue to try to control your own life? Or will you surrender your life to God? The choice is yours.

If you only knew what you were made for . . .